1,001
Country Home
Tips & Tricks

Household Hints for Cleaning, Gardening, Cooking, Sewing, and More

Mary Rose Quigg

Skyhorse Publishing

Skyhorse Publishing books may be purchased in bulk at special discounts for sales promotion, corporate gifts, fund-raising, or educational purposes. Special editions can also be created to specifications. For details, contact the Special Sales Department, Skyhorse Publishing, 307 West 36th Street, 11th Floor, New York, NY 10018 or info@skyhorsepublishing.com.

Skyhorse® and Skyhorse Publishing® are registered trademarks of Skyhorse Publishing, Inc.®, a Delaware corporation.

Visit our website at www.skyhorsepublishing.com.

10 9 8 7 6 5 4 3 2 1

Library of Congress Cataloging-in-Publication Data is available on file.

Cover design by Daniel Brount
Cover image by Shutterstock

Print ISBN: 978-1-5107-6224-4
Ebook ISBN: 978-1-5107-6633-4

Printed in China

I would like to dedicate this book to my mother Mary Heron. She loved hints books and I know she would have been very proud of this one. A big thank you to Joe, Karen, Arleen, Orla, Cathal, and Brenda for their encouragement and support.

Sweet
Home

Contents

Introduction

"Efficiency means accomplishing more with less exertion and less expense."

This comprehensive collection of over one thousand valuable hints and tips has been compiled to help make daily tasks easier and less expensive. Over the years I have accumulated hundreds of household hints and tips. Many were given to me by my mother and friends; others have come from my own experience as a cook and housewife.

Cooking, baking, household chores, laundry, stain removal, D.I.Y., and gardening are the main subjects covered but you will find much more of interest, especially the proverbs and sayings that have given me pleasure over the years. Throughout the book, I recommend natural, environmentally friendly products whenever appropriate.

Working on this book has been a labor of love; I have gotten such great enjoyment from sorting and arranging the hints, tips, and ideas into a practical book. I hope you find it interesting and entertaining, but most of all I hope that it is useful to you and improves the quality of your daily life.

—MARY ROSE

Snacks and Baking

SNACKS

For a tasty snack, toast a slice of bread on one side. Turn over and spread with tomato purée, top with grated cheese, and pop under the broiler. Add cooked bacon, mushrooms, or any other topping.

• • • •

Cover a split pita bread with tomato purée, top with cheese, and place under the broiler for a few minutes.

• • • •

For a delicious beef sandwich: Place beef on a slice of bread and spread with a little horseradish. Sprinkle some crumbled cheese and onion crisps over and place another slice of bread on top. Cut into quarters.

• • • •

Core a large cooking apple. Stuff the center with pork sausage. Bake at 350°F. When cooked, cover with a thin slice of cheese, season, and brown under the broiler.

• • • •

A dip for fruit or vegetables: Whip half a small carton of heavy cream to soft peaks, then stir in half a carton of natural yogurt. Add a pinch of salt, one teaspoon of mayonnaise, and two tablespoons crunchy peanut butter.

"If bread is the first necessity of life, recreation is a close second."
—Edward Bellamy

Mince some leftover chicken or ham, season, add a few drops of Tabasco or some other sauce, and mix with mayonnaise. Spread on slices of hot, buttered toast.

. . . .

Roll out a square of puff pastry. Cover with a layer of creamed mashed potato and a layer of grated cheese. Roll up like a Swiss roll and cut into slices. Bake at 400°F until golden. Serve hot or cold.

DAIRY PRODUCTS

If Greek yogurt is unavailable, mix a carton of low-fat natural yogurt and a carton of heavy cream together.

. . . .

Add 1 teaspoon (5 milliliters) crushed instant coffee granules to cream before whipping for an excellent topping for bananas or ice cream.

. . . .

Store containers of sour cream upside down in the refrigerator to keep fresh longer.

. . . .

Pipe unused fresh whipped cream into rosettes on a baking tray and freeze for dessert decoration.

. . . .

Freeze leftover fresh cream in ice cube trays, put into a plastic bag when frozen, and use in soups as required.

. . . .

To keep cream fresh for longer, add one teaspoon of brandy to the carton.

. . . .

Maximize the sherry taste in a trifle by adding most of the sherry to the cream and the remainder to the sponge.

. . . .

To stop milk from boiling over, rub buttered paper around the inside of the top of the saucepan. Or place a wooden spoon in the pan just before the milk comes to a boil.

. . . .

If an excess purchase of milk is near its sell-by date, make a cheese or white sauce and freeze to use later.

. . . .

Freeze fresh milk in an ice cube tray to use as a standby if you run out.

. . . .

Add a pinch of salt to milk to keep it fresh longer.

. . . .

Always rinse milk jugs or bottles thoroughly in cold water before washing as usual.

. . . .

Never pour room temperature milk or cream back into the original container.

. . . .

To keep condensed milk fresh, empty the contents of a newly opened can into a screw-top jar and store in the refrigerator.

. . . .

Add two drops of vanilla extract to 1 pint (600 milliliters) of reconstituted dried milk to give it a "fresh" taste.

. . . .

Add the juice of half a lemon to a small can of chilled evaporated milk and it can be whipped until stiff.

. . . .

Make an instant smoothie by whisking half a carton of fruit-flavored yogurt into half a glass of cold milk.

. . . .

Budget butter: take ¼ lb butter, ¼ lb margarine, 1 large egg, and ¼ pint slightly warmed milk. Using an electric mixer, put the butter and margarine into a bowl and mix until well creamed. Add the egg and beat well, then slowly add the milk with the mixer running. Leave to cool before using. This will produce 1¼ lb butter.

. . . .

If you need unsalted butter, cut salted butter into small cubes and pour boiling water over them. When melted, chill in the refrigerator. When the butter resets the salt will be in the water.

. . . .

Before unwrapping butter or margarine, run cold water over the packet for a few seconds and the contents will come away cleanly.

. . . .

Wrap cheese in plastic film or foil, except for traditional cheese with rind, which should be wrapped in greaseproof paper.

. . . .

Cheese should be stored covered in the salad compartment or door of the refrigerator.

. . . .

If you like using Edam cheese because of its low fat but do not like the texture, freeze it, and after a week it will be crumbly with a strong flavor.

. . . .

"Everyone is kneaded out of the same dough but not baked in the same oven."
—Yiddish Proverb

Mature hard cheese can be frozen, although the texture and taste can be slightly affected. Crumblier varieties tend not to freeze well as they tend to break up when defrosted. They can be used for cooking.

· · · ·

To soften cheese that has gone hard, soak a cloth in some white wine, squeeze it out, and wrap it around the cheese. Leave for several hours.

· · · ·

Make dried-out cheese into a spread by grating, adding cream and mustard, and beating well.

· · · ·

Run cold water over your cheese grater before use and it will be easier to clean.

· · · ·

Grate leftover pieces of hard cheese and store in a plastic bag in the refrigerator or freezer. They are useful for sauces, sprinkling on "au gratin" dishes or soup, or for sandwich fillings.

· · · ·

To keep cheese fresher longer and prevent it from becoming moldy, wrap in a cloth dampened with vinegar or saltwater. Or keep a sugar lump in the cheese box.

· · · ·

Smear a little butter or margarine along the cut edge of a piece of cheese before re-wrapping and storing in the refrigerator to keep it from becoming hard and waxy.

. . . .

Use an apple peeler to cut wafer thin slices of cheese for serving in a salad bowl.

. . . .

Store the cottage cheese container upside down and it will stay fresher longer.

FOOD HINTS

Keep fresh coffee in the refrigerator or freezer to preserve the flavor.

. . . .

A good substitute for coffee filter paper is two layers of kitchen paper towels.

. . . .

Store tea in an airtight tin away from strong smells as it attracts moisture and smells. Loose tea will retain its flavor for six months and tea bags for four months.

. . . .

Remove the small bits of cornflakes from the bottom of the box by sieving the cereal in a colander.

. . . .

If milk boils over, sprinkle plenty of salt on it immediately and brush off. This eliminates that awful burning smell.

• • • •

Fill a shaker with three-quarters salt to one-quarter ground black pepper and use to season when cooking.

• • • •

Bread will keep up to three weeks in a refrigerator if wrapped in foil and put on a low shelf.

• • • •

If you haven't finished a bottle of champagne or sparkling wine, pop a teaspoon handle down into the neck of the bottle. The wine will keep until the next day without losing its fizz.

• • • •

Keep the fizz in a plastic seltzer bottle by squeezing the bottle before closing.

• • • •

Cut a complete strip from the top of frozen food bags and use as a tie when returning the bag to the freezer.

. . . .

Place cans of baked beans or soup upside down when storing to avoid the liquid settling at the top.

. . . .

If a pan of boiling water or milk is about to boil over, quickly pop a metal spoon into it and this will immediately reduce the bubbling.

. . . .

Instead of sewing up a stuffed chicken, just close the neck flap with a cocktail stick.

EGGS

Fresh eggs should be heavy for size and have a rough and chalky shell. Old eggs are smooth and shiny.

. . . .

Remove eggs from the refrigerator about an hour before use. It is important to have eggs at room temperature when using for baking. Cold eggs are more likely to crack when boiled and cold egg whites are not easily whipped.

. . . .

When separating egg yolk from white, ensure that there is no yolk in the white as the whisked volume will be less.

. . . .

To easily separate an egg, crack the egg into a cup, tip it into the palm of your hand, and allow the white to slip through your fingers. Or crack the egg gently on to a saucer, hold the yolk in place with an egg cup, and drain off the white.

. . . .

If some egg yolk gets into the egg white when separating eggs, remove the yolk by holding a small clean cloth wrung out in hot water near the yolk. It acts like a magnet and draws out the yolk.

. . . .

To keep spare egg whites, put into a jar, cover with a lid, and keep in the refrigerator. Use for meringues within two weeks. Four egg whites measure around ¼ pint (150 milliliters). Egg whites can also be frozen, but use them after a few weeks.

. . . .

The easiest way to remove eggshell from a bowl after cracking an egg is with a piece of bread. The shell sticks to the bread immediately.

. . . .

Egg whites thicken up faster when beating them with an added pinch of salt.

. . . .

A pinch of cornstarch and a pinch of sugar added to the egg before beating will stop omelettes from collapsing when cooked.

. . . .

An omelette will be lighter if two teaspoons of water are added for each egg used. Beat the eggs only enough to mix them; over-beating will produce a tough omelette. Or add a dash of soda water to the beaten egg mixture and they will turn out light and fluffy.

. . . .

When making scrambled eggs for a large crowd, add a pinch of baking powder and 2 teaspoons (10 milliliters) water for each egg. Or add a dash of fizzy mineral water.

. . . .

A squeeze of lemon added to eggs while being scrambled helps to bring out the flavor.

. . . .

Place eggs for poaching in boiling water for a few seconds before cracking the shells and this will prevent the yolk from breaking.

. . . .

When poaching eggs, put a pinch of salt and a small piece of butter or a tablespoon of oil into the water and the eggs will not stick to the pan.

. . . .

Avoid splattering and sticking when frying by heating the pan before adding the butter or oil. This even prevents eggs from sticking.

• • • •

To hard-boil eggs, heat the water before adding the eggs, bring to a boil, and then gently boil for eight to ten minutes. Pour off the hot water and crack the egg gently under a cold running tap. Leave the shelled eggs in a bowl of cold water until ready to use.

• • • •

If boiled eggs are too runny for making sandwiches, finely crumble some dry bread in a processor or on a grater and add to the egg for a perfect filling.

• • • •

To slice hard-boiled eggs, dip a knife in boiling water and dry before using the knife. The eggs will not break or crumble.

• • • •

When several hard-boiled eggs are required for sandwiches, put them in a bowl with butter, salt, and pepper and mash with a potato masher.

• • • •

When surplus eggs are close to their use-by date, hard-boil them and allow to cool. Pickle them in vinegar and they'll taste delicious and last for weeks.

• • • •

If an egg breaks on the floor, cover it with salt (this will absorb most of the slippery white) and it will clean up easily with a damp cloth.

SWEET & STICKY FOOD

To weigh out honey or syrup, put the tin on the scales and take out spoonfuls until the weight has reduced by the amount you require. Or coat the scale pan with flour before adding the syrup; it will tip out quite easily.

• • • •

Coat a metal spoon with cooking oil before measuring out honey or syrup; it will slip off easily. Or heat the spoon.

• • • •

Remove the syrup from glacé cherries by placing them in a sieve and rinsing under running water. Drain and dry well with kitchen paper.

• • • •

Stiff honey can be made runny again by placing the jar in a bowl of warm water or heating in the microwave for a few seconds.

• • • •

To make caramel: Dissolve 4 ounces (100 grams) granulated sugar in 4 tablespoons (60 milliliters) water. Boil over a steady heat, without stirring, until golden brown.

• • • •

Add lemon juice to the mix when making toffee, to keep it from hardening in the pan.

• • • •

When melting chocolate, grease the inside of the pan thoroughly to prevent it sticking to the sides and bottom.

. . . .

If you run out of chocolate when baking, replace with a mixture of 4 tablespoons (60 milliliters) cocoa combined with 1 teaspoon (5 milliliters) melted butter.

. . . .

When melting chocolate, place it in a stainless steel pan in the oven with the buns or cake and it will be ready when they are cooked. It also helps to grease the sides and bottom of the container to prevent sticking and waste.

. . . .

If you run out of brown sugar when baking, use white sugar and molasses instead. For every 8 ounces (225 grams) sugar add 1 tablespoon (15 milliliters) molasses for light brown sugar and 2 tablespoons (30 milliliters) for dark brown sugar.

. . . .

To soften solid lumps of sugar to speed up creaming of butter and sugar, place sugar in the microwave for a few seconds.

• • • •

Soft brown sugar can go hard when stored. Ways to soften it are:
- Place it in a jar and put in a washed lemon.
- Put sugar into a bowl and cover with a fairly damp tea towel for a few hours or overnight.
- Add a slice of soft bread to the package and seal tightly for a few hours.
- If needed in a hurry, grate the hard block of sugar.

• • • •

To make candied citrus peel: the peel of three oranges or lemons should be soaked for three days in 1 pint (600 milliliters) water with 2 tablespoons (30 milliliters) of added salt. Remove the pieces of peel and dry carefully. Next make a syrup of ½ pint (300 milliliters) water and 8 ounces (225 grams) sugar, add the peel, and allow to simmer for two hours. Remove each piece and coat with fine sugar.

• • • •

Before using citrus fruits, pare off the rind with a potato peeler, cut into small pieces, put in a screw-top jar, cover with golden syrup, and mix well. Delicious if added to cakes.

• • • •

Use a wet knife to cut crystallized ginger or other glacé fruits.

• • • •

Put root ginger into the freezer immediately after purchase. When required, grate the required amount and return the remainder to the freezer.

• • • •

Peel root ginger and store in a jar of sherry. This will preserve it and the sherry can be used in stir-fries.

• • • •

Nutmeg is easier to grate if soaked in hot water for a few minutes.

• • • •

Put orange peel on a sheet pan lined with parchment paper and bake at 95°F for about 2 hours or until crisp. Then crush to powder and store in a jar. Small amounts added to cake mixtures give a lovely flavor.

PASTRY

Add 1 teaspoon (5 milliliters) of Worcestershire sauce to piecrust pastry used for savory dishes.

• • • •

Use soda water when mixing piecrust pastry to give it a light texture.

• • • •

"The hardness of the butter is proportional to the softness of the bread "
—Steven Wright

When making sweet pastry, work in a little vanilla extract into the butter or shortening before rubbing in the flour.

• • • •

The secret of good pastry is to keep ingredients and cooking implements cool. Always rest the dough in the refrigerator for at least half an hour before rolling out.

• • • •

To ensure pastry is light, make the dough with the yolk of an egg and 1 tablespoon (15 milliliters) of lemon juice.

• • • •

When rolling out sweet pastry for pies, sprinkle the work surface with cornstarch.

• • • •

To avoid pastry sticking, roll out between two pieces of plastic wrap. There is no need to use extra flour or greaseproof paper and it can be easily turned around.

• • • •

If you tend to over-stretch pastry, leave some surplus around the edge when you trim the pastry. Leave in a cool place for half an hour before using.

• • • •

Brush bottom piecrusts with egg white before adding any filling to keep it from soaking into the base.

. . . .

Roll out leftover pastry and cut into circles. Interleave with greaseproof paper and freeze. When required, just thaw and line pie plates.

. . . .

For a crispy crust on pastry, brush lightly with cold milk or water. Shake with superfine sugar for a sweet filling.

. . . .

Run cold water over the baking tray before laying puff pastry on it. When the tin is heated the water will steam and help the pastry to puff up. Or place an ovenproof bowl of hot water in the bottom of the oven while baking.

BREAD & BATTER

When making yeast bread, add 1 teaspoon (5 milliliters) cider vinegar per 1 lb (450 grams) flour for improved fermentation and texture.

. . . .

If bread is wrapped in foil and put on the lower shelf of a refrigerator it will keep for up to three weeks.

. . . .

To freshen stale bread, wrap the bread in a cloth dipped in hot water. When the crust is moist and soft, place it in a moderately hot oven until the crust is crisp.

. . . .

"In the childhood memories of every good cook, there's a large kitchen, a warm stove, a simmering pot, and a mom."
—Barbara Costikyan

If you live alone, instead of freezing a whole loaf of bread, make packages of four to six slices so you can defrost small amounts at a time.

• • • •

To avoid waste, cut the crusts off the bread before making sandwiches. They can be cut into cubes and deep fried to make croutons, or made into breadcrumbs.

• • • •

For stuffing, soak cubes of bread in water or milk, squeeze out the excess liquid, and crumble the bread.

• • • •

To make toasted breadcrumbs without a processor, toast thin slices of bread, put them in a plastic bag, and roll with a rolling pin.

• • • •

To make flavored croutons, fry small cubes of bread in hot oil until crispy and golden. Place a couple of peeled garlic cloves or a bunch of herbs in a greaseproof paper bag, add the croutons and seal the bag. Use when cool.

. . . .

For a really crisp batter on fried fish: Make your usual batter and leave to stand for 20 minutes. Meanwhile put 1 tablespoon (15 milliliters) warm water, 1 teaspoon (5 milliliters) sugar, and ¼ teaspoon (1.25 milliliters) dried yeast in a cup and stand in a warm place. When ready to use the batter, stir in the yeast mixture.

. . . .

Add 1 tablespoon (15 milliliters) vinegar or a dash of beer into batter for fish to make it brown and crispy.

. . . .

CAKES

If you require cake flour but only have all-purpose flour, just sift the flour about five times.

. . . .

To prevent cake mixes from curdling, add a little sifted flour when beating in the eggs.

. . . .

When folding egg whites into a cake mixture, first stir in a large spoonful to lighten it and then it will be easier to blend in the remainder.

. . . .

Sponge cakes are cooked if the sides of the cake have shrunk from the tin. Or press the center of the cake lightly and it should spring back immediately. If you can hear the cake "sizzling," it is not quite cooked.

. . . .

A sponge cake will be easier to remove from the tin if it is placed on a damp cloth for a minute before turning out.

. . . .

Chocolate cakes should be well risen and often they are slightly cracked in the center. Always leave them in the tin for five minutes before turning out on the cooling tray.

. . . .

Cover fruit cakes with greaseproof paper half way through baking to avoid the top becoming burnt.

. . . .

Test fruit cakes by piercing the center of the cake with a metal skewer. If the cake is done, the skewer should come out clean.

. . . .

When creaming butter and sugar together, add a tablespoon of boiling water for a lighter cake.

. . . .

When adding coffee granules to a mixture, always dissolve them in a little water first and they will blend into the mixture more easily.

. . . .

When adding any flavoring—such as vanilla—to a cake, mix it with the beaten egg to ensure even distribution.

. . . .

Use strong, black, cold coffee instead of milk when making gingerbread, spiced fruit cake, or chocolate pudding to give a delicious flavor and dark color.

. . . .

To have a flat top when cooked, hollow out the center of a rich fruit cake before putting it in the oven.

. . . .

To keep cakes moist and stop them cracking when you bake them, put a dish of water in the bottom of the oven. Or lightly brush the top with water before baking.

. . . .

When spreading jam or cream on a sponge or meringue, use the back of a spoon instead of a knife.

. . . .

For a crispy topping on a sponge cake, crush a cup of breakfast cereal and mix with a tablespoon of jam. Spread over the uncooked cake and bake as usual.

• • • •

Make sure that the fruit is evenly distributed in a cake by shaking the dried fruit in a paper bag with a little flour before adding it to the cake batter.

• • • •

Add 1 ounce (25 grams) custard powder to your favorite fruit cake mix and it will turn out golden inside. Or add 1 tablespoon (15 milliliters) peanut butter for a nutty taste.

• • • •

In a cake recipe where dried fruit is soaked in tea or coffee, try using an herbal infusion instead. Try hibiscus, rosehip, or lemon for a lovely change.

• • • •

Instead of dried fruit, add half a jar of mincemeat to your usual cake recipe to make a deliciously moist cake.

. . . .

Sift ¼ teaspoon (1.25 milliliters) dry mustard with each 8 ounces (225 grams) flour when baking rich fruit cakes. This helps to develop a mellow fruity flavor.

. . . .

If you don't like candied peel in a fruit cake, add 1 tablespoon (15 milliliters) each of orange and lemon marmalade for flavor and moistness.

. . . .

When making fruit cakes or scones, soak the dried fruit in pure apple or orange juice for a lovely flavor.

. . . .

When making a fruit loaf, soak the fruit in hot tea for half an hour instead of overnight.

. . . .

When a cake recipe requires chopped nuts, substitute them with sunflower seeds.

COOKIES & BUNS

Roll cookie dough into a long sausage and slice thinly instead of cutting individually into circles.

. . . .

Always use a shallow baking tray when baking cookies so that they will brown evenly.

• • • •

Make your usual shortbread recipe. Melt a Mars Bar and spread over the top. Leave to harden before slicing.

• • • •

Add a little custard powder to the mix when making shortbread, scones, or cookies to give a lovely creamy taste.

• • • •

For crispier cookies, use half margarine and half lard in the mixture. Or substitute 1 ounce (25 grams) flour for cornstarch.

• • • •

To make frosted cookies, remove them from the oven just before they are cooked. Brush with beaten egg white and dust with sugar and return to the oven.

• • • •

Place a sugar lump in the cookie tin to keep them crisp.

• • • •

Cookies stay fresher if you place crumpled tissue paper in the bottom of the storage jar.

• • • •

Use ginger cookies instead of sponges at the bottom of a trifle.

• • • •

"An apple is an excellent thing—until you have tried a peach."
—Unknown

Make sure jam tarts don't boil over during baking by sprinkling a few drops of water on the jam.

. . . .

When making buns or cakes, add 2 teaspoons (10 milliliters) of apple purée to the mix—it improves the taste.

. . . .

When making cupcakes, add 2 tablespoons (30 milliliters) of semolina to every 8 ounces (225 grams) of flour to give a lovely texture.

. . . .

Use olive oil to grease tins or mixing bowls and the mixture will never stick.

FROSTING & FILLINGS

Sprinkle a little flour over the top of a cake before icing. It will keep the icing from slipping over the edge or down the sides.

. . . .

Add a pinch of baking soda to frosting and it will stay moist and prevent cracking.

. . . .

When making lemon icing, add 2 teaspoons (10 milliliters) custard powder to ½ pound (225 grams) icing sugar and mix with the juice of a lemon.

. . . .

For a quick chocolate icing, sprinkle grated chocolate over the top of the cake and place under a medium broiler for a couple of minutes. Spread evenly.

· · · ·

A substitute for chocolate frosting can be made by combining sweetened condensed milk with powdered cocoa until frosting consistency is reached.

· · · ·

For an unusual icing effect on a cake, put two different colors of icing into one bag, one down each side. The colors will twist and blend.

· · · ·

To make coffee essence for adding to sauces or icing, dissolve 1 tablespoon (15 milliliters) instant coffee granules in 2 teaspoons (10 milliliters) boiling water.

· · · ·

Scrape a chocolate bar with a potato peeler to make fine decorative curls for topping cakes and trifles.

. . . .

When putting a jam sponge together, spread each half lightly with soft margarine or cooled melted butter. It stops the jam from soaking into the sponge.

. . . .

Lemon filling for a sponge cake or flan: lightly whip ⅓ pint (200 milliliters) heavy cream, then fold in 2 tablespoons (30 milliliters) lemon curd. Use as filling, chill overnight.

. . . .

Buttercream frosting will keep for up to three weeks in a covered container in the refrigerator. Make up a large quantity without flavorings and use them as needed.

DELICIOUS DESSERT

For a nutty taste when making a fruit crumble, substitute 1 ounce (25 grams) flour with desiccated coconut. Add 1 tablespoon (15 milliliters) of ground almonds or coconut to give extra flavor.

. . . .

Add demerara sugar instead of granulated to the topping of a fruit crumble to add a little crunch.

. . . .

Top ordinary bread and butter pudding with meringue and return to oven at 400°F for ten minutes. When making bread and butter pudding, try using lemon curd instead of butter.

. . . .

Grate a cooking apple over the dried fruit when making bread and butter pudding.

. . . .

Add two teaspoons of coffee creamer when making instant custard for a creamier texture.

. . . .

Lightly sprinkle apple slices with plain flour when making a tart. As the apples soften, the flour acts as a thickening agent.

. . . .

When making fruit pies, put the sugar between two layers of fruit and the juice won't boil over.

. . . .

Add zip to apple pie by squeezing fresh orange juice over each layer of apple before cooking.

Put a layer of lemon curd on the bottom of an apple tart to give a lovely flavor.

. . . .

Before putting the top crust on an apple tart, cover the apples with a layer of bananas.

. . . .

When baking apples, use a small piece of marzipan to plug the bottom and stop the filling from escaping. Or stand each apple in a foil dish and place on a baking tray.

. . . .

Crush seven or eight gingersnaps into 2 ounces (50 grams) melted butter. Mix thoroughly and spread over a cooked rice pudding. Return pudding to the oven for a few minutes.

. . . .

Cover trifles with a mixture of crushed meringue shells and whipped cream. Grate chocolate over the top.

. . . .

Whole seedless grapes set in a lime Jell-O and topped with whipped cream makes a refreshing pudding.

. . . .

For a tasty dessert: place some peach halves (cut side up) on a grill pan. Top each peach with halved marshmallows and heat on the grill or under the broiler until the marshmallows begin to melt and turn golden brown.

. . . .

Make a sauce for fruit salad by whipping a small carton of heavy cream until thick, add 2 tablespoons (30 milliliters) honey, and mix well. Stir in 1 tablespoon (15 milliliters) lemon juice.

MOUTH WATERING MERINGUES

To make sure that egg whites whisk well, the bowl and beaters have to be free from all traces of grease. Wash the bowl and beaters in warm soapy water, rinse, and dry well. Then rub a little lemon juice around the bowl.

. . . .

To get the best volume from whipped egg whites, have the eggs, bowl, and beaters all at room temperature.

. . . .

Add 1 teaspoon (5 milliliters) cream of tartar to every four egg whites to produce larger, crisp, dry meringues.

. . . .

When making meringues, 1 teaspoon (5 milliliters) cornstarch added to 4 ounces (100 grams) sugar prevents a "toffee" consistency from forming.

. . . .

Egg whites are whisked sufficiently when the mixing bowl can be held upside down without the contents falling out.

"I never worry about diets. The only carrots that interest me are the number you get in a diamond."
—Mae West

Whisk egg whites well between each addition of superfine sugar. If this is not done, the cooked meringue will weep and a syrupy liquid will appear on the surface.

. . . .

For snowy white meringue, add a drop of distilled malt vinegar to the egg white before starting to whisk.

. . . .

For coffee meringues, add 1 teaspoon (5 milliliters) coffee essence per egg white after all the superfine sugar has been added.

. . . .

To keep whisked egg whites stiff for up to half an hour, cover the bowl with plastic wrap or tin foil so that it is airtight.

. . . .

To stop meringue from shrinking away from the sides of pies, make sure it touches the pastry all around the edge. It will bake onto the pastry and not shrink.

. . . .

To cut smoothly into a lemon meringue pie, grease both sides of the knife with margarine or butter.

. . . .

Cook meringues in a slow oven. If the temperature is too high, the sugar will weep out as a syrup and the meringues will be golden colored.

. . . .

To store meringues, cool thoroughly and wrap in foil or arrange in an airtight tin with greaseproof paper between each layer. They will keep for two months.

FOOD HINTS

Use disposable gloves while kneading dough.

· · · ·

To save switching on the oven to heat and crisp breakfast rolls or croissants, put them instead in a heavy saucepan or frying pan with a tight fitting lid and heat on the stovetop for a few minutes.

· · · ·

Pour half a new bottle of vinegar into an empty vinegar bottle. Top up both bottles with cooled boiled water. Leave for 24 hours. The vinegar regains its strength so you have two bottles for the price of one.

· · · ·

To restore the flavor to spices that have been stored for a while, pour out of the jar and roast in the oven on a high heat. Remove from the oven as soon as you smell their aroma.

· · · ·

Making breadcrumbs from fresh bread can be difficult. For dry crumbs, dip the bread in flour, shake off the surplus, and then whizz in a blender. For bread sauce or puddings, pour a little water over the bread and mash with a fork.

. . . .

Use a spare eyedropper to dispense food coloring or flavoring.

. . . .

After a baking session, rinse floury tins, cutlery, or boards in cold water first. Hot water makes flour stickier and more difficult to remove.

. . . .

Put a clean potato in the bread bin to keep bread fresh. Or add a rib of celery to the bread bag.

. . . .

To make self-rising flour, add 2½ teaspoons (12.5 milliliters) baking powder to every 8 ounces (225 grams) all-purpose flour. (For scones, add 3 teaspoons (15 milliliters) baking powder). Or instead of baking powder use ½ teaspoon (2.5 milliliters) baking soda and 1 teaspoon (5 milliliters) cream of tartar sifted together several times.

. . . .

To prevent the outside of a rich cake from burning, place the cake tin inside a slightly larger one before baking in the oven.

. . . .

To cut a pie or flan into five equal parts, cut a Y in the pie and then cut the larger pieces in half.

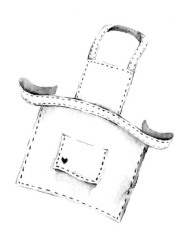

Culinary Aids

COOKING TIPS

When mixing dry mustard powder, use milk or olive oil instead of water. They improve the flavor and won't dry out so quickly. Beer or whiskey will give the mustard a tangy taste.

. . . .

A pinch of mustard added to percolating coffee brings out the flavor.

. . . .

To make seasoned flour, for every 4 ounces (100 grams) plain flour, add 2 teaspoons (10 milliliters) salt and ½ teaspoon (2.5 milliliters) pepper.

. . . .

Before making oatmeal, lightly rub the inside of the saucepan with butter. It will be much easier to clean afterwards.

. . . .

Make oatmeal creamier by adding a spoonful of vanilla ice cream during cooking.

. . . .

Make Thousand Island dressing by adding a little tomato purée to mayonnaise.

. . . .

Instead of salad dressing, use plain yogurt with a little paprika and lemon juice added.

. . . .

For a refreshing salad dressing, add 1 teaspoon (5 milliliters)
each of lemon curd, mayonnaise, and chopped chives
to a carton of plain yogurt.

• • • •

Make crisp fried bread by spreading butter or margarine lightly
on each side of the slice and then frying in a dry pan until golden
brown on both sides.

• • • •

To use up stale French bread, slice it up, spread with garlic butter,
wrap, and freeze. Put into the oven for a few minutes when you
want garlic bread.

Add a pat of butter when cooking baked beans
and they won't stick.

• • • •

To prevent butter burning when frying with butter, add a little
cooking oil to the melting butter.

• • • •

Rinse uncooked rice several times to remove excess starch. Also avoid stirring the rice during cooking. Add a teaspoon of oil or butter or a few drops of lemon juice.

. . . .

Use turmeric instead of saffron to color rice yellow.

. . . .

To reduce the acidity of tomato-based pasta sauces, add some grated or chopped carrots.

. . . .

If a main dish or vegetable is too sweet, add 1 teaspoon (5 milliliters) of cider vinegar.

. . . .

For a quick gravy thickener, add some instant potatoes.

. . . .

To separate frozen bacon, heat a metal spatula over the stove burner and slide under each slice.

. . . .

To prevent bacon from curling, dip the strips in cold water before cooking.

. . . .

Mash in 1–2 teaspoons (5–10 milliliters) wholegrain mustard instead of butter to have tasty, low calorie mashed potato.

. . . .

"A stomach that is seldom empty despises common food."
—*Unknown*

Add 2 teaspoons (10 milliliters) cinnamon for extra tasty spaghetti Bolognese.

• • • •

Keep a supply of roux mix in the fridge. Put 8 ounces (225 grams) butter or margarine and 8 ounces (225 grams) all-purpose flour in a saucepan, and stir over a gentle heat until crumbly. Do not allow to burn. Cool and store in a screw topped jar in the fridge. When making a sauce, heat ½ pint (300 milliliters) milk and add 2 tablespoons (30 milliliters) of the roux, and beat well until smooth. Add cheese or parsley as required.

• • • •

Put canned meat in the refrigerator for a few hours before opening. The chilled meat will be easier to slice.

• • • •

When making a casserole, butter the inside of the dish before adding the meat and vegetables. The food won't stick to the dish and the dish will be easier to clean.

• • • •

Defrost frozen foods quickly by placing on a cooling rack.

SOUP & SAVORY SAUCES

Adding a boiled potato or a crustless slice or two of bread to a thin soup and whirring in the blender will make the soup velvety immediately.

. . . .

Always season soups or stews towards the end of cooking, when the liquid has been reduced.

. . . .

Add a raw potato to over-salted soup and simmer for ten minutes.

. . . .

To avoid pea soup turning into pease pudding, add cornstarch or roux to stabilize the proteins and keep the liquid at the required consistency.

. . . .

Add some of the papery outer onion skin to a broth liquid to make it a lovely golden color. Strain before using the broth.

. . . .

Add 1 tablespoon (15 milliliters) prune juice to soups to enrich their flavor and color. A lump of sugar added to clear soup will improve its appearance.

. . . .

When making stock from beef or chicken bones, place the bones in a fry basket in the saucepan and they will be easily removed.

. . . .

Before making stock from meat bones, grill the bones until brown and the stock will have a richer color.

. . . .

When cooking a chicken carcass or meat bones for stock, always keep at a gentle simmer as fast boiling will make the stock cloudy.

. . . .

A certain amount of scum will rise to the surface when cooking stock. Skim away frequently by sliding a large spoon horizontally across the surface; gently lift off the scum and discard.

. . . .

To remove fat from stock, allow to cool for 30 minutes, then skim off as above. To de-grease more thoroughly, leave to cool overnight and remove the solidified fat in the morning.

. . . .

Don't waste a little leftover wine; pour it into an ice cube tray and freeze it. When making a stew or soup, add the cubes for improved flavor.

. . . .

Use empty milk or fruit juice cartons to freeze soup or gravy. Cut the top off the carton, line with a plastic bag, and fill. When frozen, pull out the bag, label, and stack in the freezer.

. . . .

Before freezing soups or stews, push a plastic cup into the middle of the food in the container and remove when the food is frozen. This hole in the center will reduce the defrosting time.

. . . .

To thicken gravy for roasts or stews, grate a small potato into it and simmer for fifteen minutes before serving.

. . . .

For a smooth mixture, try adding warm milk instead of cold when making white sauce.

. . . .

For an instant white sauce, blend together 1 cup soft butter and 1 cup flour. Spread it in an ice cube tray and chill well. Cut into 16 cubes before storing in a freezer bag. For medium-thick sauce, drop 1 cube in 1 cup milk and heat slowly, stirring as it thickens.

. . . .

If a sauce curdles or separates after the addition of cream, remove from the heat and add a few ice cubes. Whisk well and the sauce will uncurdle.

. . . .

Make a speedy parsley sauce by mixing together 2 teaspoons (10 milliliters) cornstarch, a pinch of salt and pepper, ½ teaspoon (2.5 milliliters) onion or garlic salt, a pat of butter, ½ pint (300 milliliters) milk, and 1 teaspoon (5 milliliters) dried parsley. Do not add the chopped parsley until the sauce has boiled. The parsley will then retain its color and freshness.

. . . .

If Hollandaise begins to curdle, drop in a couple of ice cubes and whisk well.

. . . .

A quick way to make a substitute tartar sauce is by combining 7 tablespoons (105 milliliters) mayonnaise with 2 tablespoons (30 milliliters) chopped mixed pickles.

BEEF & LAMB

Frozen meat is best thawed slowly in the refrigerator. However, in an emergency it can be thawed quickly by immersing in cold water with a handful of salt added. Soak for 30 minutes, rinse well, and pat dry.

. . . .

Do not add salt to ground beef at the start of cooking as the meat tends to go rubbery.

. . . .

"A tale without love is like beef without mustard, an insipid dish."
—Unknown

After cooking ground beef, place a slice of bread on top and it will soak up the fat.

. . . .

As a variation on a potato topping on shepherd's pie, butter some slices of white bread, cut into 1-inch (2.5 centimeters) squares, and arrange on top. Sprinkle with grated cheese and bake as usual. Or cover with cooked noodles and sprinkle with grated cheese.

. . . .

Meatballs and hamburgers are shaped more easily with wet hands.

. . . .

Tenderize boiled meat by adding a tablespoon of vinegar to the cooking water.

. . . .

Tenderize steak by rubbing a mixture of equal parts malt vinegar and cooking or olive oil into the surface and allow to stand for two hours.

. . . .

When tenderizing meat with a mallet or rolling pin, sprinkle a little water on both the mallet and the work surface to stop the meat sticking to either.

. . . .

When grilling meat on a rack, place a slice of bread in the grill pan to eliminate the smoking fat and reduce the fire risk.

. . . .

Before putting the pastry topping on a meat pie, grate a little potato on top of the meat to thicken the gravy.

. . . .

When putting a top crust on meat or fish pies, place an eggcup upside down in the center of the filling to keep the lid up when the filling shrinks during cooking.

. . . .

Instead of a top crust on a pie, try a vegetable topping. Grate a raw carrot, raw parsnip, and a little raw rutabaga, then add two cups of cold mashed potato, 2 tablespoons (30 milliliters) of melted butter, and seasoning to taste. Mix well and use to cover the pie. Bake for one hour at 350°F.

. . . .

Keep all clean vegetable peelings and put in the bottom of the pan when roasting meat. When the meat is cooked, pour some water over the peelings and drain off to use for a lovely flavored gravy stock.

. . . .

Place meat on a meat rack in a roasting tin and it will not burn on the bottom.

. . . .

"After a good dinner, one can forgive anybody, even one's relatives."
—Oscar Wilde

Rub the surface of meat with grainy or dry mustard powder before roasting, frying, or grilling to give a lovely flavor.

• • • •

When roasting a joint of lamb or beef, put a cup of cold water into the baking tray. This reduces shrinkage, keeps the meat succulent, and gives stock for the gravy.

• • • •

Cold meat placed in the freezer for 30 minutes can be cut into thin slices more easily.

• • • •

If you have to keep beef or lamb in the refrigerator for a few days, rub it all over with vinegar and sprinkle with chopped onion. Wipe off onion before cooking.

• • • •

Before roasting lamb, tuck bits of garlic into tiny holes in the meat to improve the flavor.

• • • •

When making lamb stew, add beer to the stock to improve the flavor.

• • • •

When inserting a meat thermometer in a joint of meat, make sure that it is not touching a bone or buried in a thick layer of fat, as this could give a misleading reading.

• • • •

Drop ice cubes or lettuce leaves into stock to easily remove excess fat—the fat will cling to them.

. . . .

For a smooth gravy, keep a jar of equal parts flour and cornstarch. When making gravy, put 3 to 4 tablespoons (45 to 60 milliliters) of this mixture into a screw-top jar, add water, and shake well. Stir the smooth paste into your gravy to thicken.

. . . .

To give extra flavor to gravy, thicken with 1 tablespoon (15 milliliters) powdered mashed potato rather than flour.

. . . .

If a pot of stew is burnt, remove from the heat, do not stir, and immediately pour the unburned portion into another saucepan. Add a raw potato or a slice of bread to absorb any burnt taste, then remove after ten minutes. Stir in a can of tomatoes to increase the quantity.

. . . .

To remove a burnt taste from stews, soup, or milk pudding, take off the heat, pour into a clean saucepan, and add a few drops of lemon juice.

PORK & POULTRY

To prevent sausage skins from bursting when frying, first prick with a fork or boil for two minutes.

. . . .

Sausage skins will peel off easily if they are held under a cold running tap for a minute.

. . . .

When grilling a lot of sausages, save time by putting them onto a skewer or long kebab stick and turning them all over together.

. . . .

Before cooking sausages on the barbecue or under the broiler, put them in a pot and cover with cold water. Bring to simmer, then remove from the water and cool under the cold tap. Dry thoroughly before cooking.

. . . .

Sausage rolls taste lovely if you spread some sweet pickle on the sausage meat before covering with pastry.

. . . .

If you find that fresh sliced ham has dried out, soak it in a little milk for ten minutes and it will regain its moisture and flavor.

. . . .

Use pineapple juice or cider to baste a pork joint or chops. This improves the flavor and appearance.

. . . .

For good crackling on pork, make narrow cuts on the skin and rub with plenty of salt. Leave refrigerated overnight, wipe off the salt, and rub the skin with cooking oil before placing in the oven.

• • • •

When defrosting frozen poultry or meat, put the unwrapped meat in a colander (or on a cake cooling tray) on a plate. It will thaw more quickly.

• • • •

To keep poultry moist when roasting in an electric oven, place a heat-proof bowl of water in the bottom of the oven while cooking.

• • • •

Improve the flavor of roast chicken by mashing 1 tablespoon (15 milliliters) dried tarragon with a large pat of butter, plus the seasoning. Put into the cavity and baste with the melted butter during cooking.

• • • •

Let a hot roast chicken stand covered with foil for ten minutes before carving. The juices settle and it carves more easily.

Roast a turkey breast side down so the juices run through and keep the breast moist.

. . . .

If you don't have a processor to make breadcrumbs, soak cubes of bread in milk or water, squeeze out the excess liquid, and crumble the bread into the stuffing mixture.

. . . .

To bring out the flavor in stuffing, add a teaspoon of mustard. Or bind with lemon juice for a different flavor.

. . . .

Grate an apple into the breadcrumb mix when making stuffing for a pork joint.

. . . .

Steep chicken pieces in milk for 30 minutes before cooking to stop them from shrinking.

. . . .

To coat chicken, meat, or fish pieces evenly with flour, place the chicken and seasoned flour in a plastic bag, seal tightly, then shake gently.

. . . .

After flouring chicken, chill for one hour. The coating adheres better during frying.

FISH

Choose plump fish of moderate size with bright eyes that are not sunken in the head. The flesh should smell pleasant, be firm, rigid, and close grained with bright red gills. The scales should be shiny and easily removed when rubbed. Inferior fish will have a bluish tinge and flabby flesh.

• • • •

Flat fish should be thick in proportion to the size.

• • • •

When purchasing a slice of fish, choose a thick slice from a small fish rather than a thin slice from a large one.

• • • •

Mackerel and herring must be very fresh.

• • • •

Sprinkle ground uncooked rice over fish before frying; this stops the fish from sticking to the pan and yields a golden brown result.

• • • •

To scale fish, first rub well with vinegar.
The scales will come off easily.

• • • •

To prevent fish slipping when skinning, dip your fingers in water and then in salt to get a good grip on the fish.

• • • •

"Fish, to taste right, must swim three
times—in water, in butter, and in wine."
—Polish Proverb

To keep a fish from falling apart when frying, first pour boiling water over it, then dry, and then fry.

. . . .

When frying fish, sprinkle a little curry powder into the pan or add to the batter. It stops the smell and improves the flavor and color.

. . . .

A few drops of vinegar added to the liquid when cooking white fish improves the texture and color.

. . . .

Add white wine, onion, carrot, parsley, dill, and seasoning to the water or stock to improve the flavor when cooking fish.

. . . .

For a quick fish dish, place fish in a casserole dish and pour over some seasoned milk. Top with a crushed packet of potato chips mixed with grated cheese. Bake in a moderate oven.

. . . .

In place of breadcrumbs for coating fish, crush some dry, cheese-flavored cookies and coat the fish with these. Or try fish dipped in beaten egg, then in crushed cornflakes.

. . . .

Top fish fillets with a mixture of mayonnaise and stiffly beaten egg whites and grill until brown.

. . . .

When baking whole fish, wrap in aluminum foil so that it can be lifted from the baking pan without the fish falling apart. To remove the foil, slip a spatula under the fish and slide the foil out after fish is on the platter.

. . . .

If you don't have a proper steamer for fish, use a metal colander over a pan and cover with the lid.

. . . .

Tuna will taste better in a salad sandwich if you first squeeze out as much oil as possible, then add one grated apple or the juice of a lemon before adding mayonnaise.

. . . .

If canned sardines tend to give you indigestion, pour off the oil and sprinkle with lemon juice.

. . . .

Vegetables and Fruits

VEGETABLE HINTS

After chopping fresh chilies, remove all traces from your hands by rubbing vegetable oil into them for a minute, then rinse off with warm soapy water.

• • • •

Put garlic cloves in boiling water for two minutes and the skin will come off easily. Or microwave them on high for 40 seconds.

• • • •

Bury peeled and pressed garlic cloves in a screw-top jar of salt. Remove the garlic after a few days and you will have a jar of low-cost seasoning.

• • • •

The way you prepare and cook garlic affects the flavor and smell. If you want a delicate flavor, leave the cloves whole or just rub around the dish with a cut clove. For a stronger taste, add chopped garlic, and for very strong flavor, crush the garlic.

• • • •

Frying garlic can make it bitter, so add it to the pan after the onion has softened or with some liquid.

*"Life expectancy would grow by leaps and bounds
if green vegetables smelled as good as bacon."*
—Doug Larson

For a sweet, mild-flavored, homemade garlic purée, boil
6–8 unpeeled cloves of garlic for ten minutes. Peel and mash
with 1 teaspoon (5 milliliters) superfine sugar and 2 teaspoons
(10 milliliters) oil.

. . . .

Add 1 teaspoon (5 milliliters) mustard to cauliflower cheese
sauce to jazz up the flavor.

. . . .

Add a bunch of parsley to the water when cooking broad beans.
It gives them color and improves the flavor.

. . . .

To avoid the unpleasant smell of cooking cauliflower, sprouts, or
cabbage, put either a slice of raw apple, a piece of toasted bread,
a squeeze of lemon juice, a few bay leaves, or a small bunch of
parsley into the cooking water—this will not alter the flavor.

. . . .

For really tasty cabbage, shred it finely, wash, and drain well.
Heat 1 tablespoon (15 milliliters) butter in a large saucepan,
add the cabbage with a sprinkle of black pepper and salt, plus a
little chopped onion and/or garlic. Cook gently for 15 minutes,
stirring occasionally.

ROOT VEGETABLES

Keep potatoes from sprouting by storing an apple with them.

. . . .

Do not use potatoes that have turned green or are well sprouted—
they taste unpleasant due to containing a mild poison

. . . .

Peel vegetables in a colander in a bowl of water and the peelings
are easily lifted out in the colander when finished.

. . . .

New potatoes are best put into boiling water to cook; however,
main-crop potatoes cook more evenly if put into cold water and
brought to a boil.

. . . .

If you must peel potatoes or Jerusalem artichokes in advance,
put them in a bowl of water with a little added cornstarch to keep
them white. Or put a slice of white bread in the bowl.

. . . .

Use the water drained from cooked potatoes for soup, gravy,
or cooking other root or green vegetables.

. . . .

Add ½ teaspoon (2.5 milliliters) dried mixed herbs to the water when
boiling potatoes to give a subtly different flavor when mashed.

. . . .

"Money is the root of all evil, and yet it is such a useful root that we cannot get on without it any more than we can without potatoes."
—*Louisa May Alcott*

To vary the flavor of mashed potato:

• • • •

Mash potatoes with plain yogurt and chopped chives.

• • • •

Substitute salad dressing or cream cheese for butter.

• • • •

Add a spoonful of pesto or a little horseradish.

• • • •

Mix the potato with mayonnaise and garlic salt, then sprinkle paprika over the top. Serve hot or cold.

• • • •

To 2 pounds (900 grams) mashed potato, add 3 tablespoons (45 milliliters) olive oil and two cloves crushed garlic.

• • • •

Boil sliced carrots and frozen peas with the potato and mash together when cooked.

• • • •

Before roasting potatoes, place them in a pan of hot water and bring to a boil. Drain and toss in oil before placing in the oven.

• • • •

For tasty roasted potatoes, cut into pieces, boil for five minutes, dip in beaten egg, roll in dry stuffing mix, and roast as usual.

. . . .

For healthier French fries, soak the potatoes in milk first. Dry well.

. . . .

Sprinkle a vegetable stock cube over oven fries before cooking to give them more flavor and texture.

. . . .

Drizzle oven fries with olive oil—experiment with flavor-infused oils if you like. To make the fries crispy, turn on the broiler for a few minutes at the end of the baking time.

. . . .

Cook baking potatoes on high in the microwave for about three to four minutes per potato before baking.

. . . .

For crispy skins on baked potatoes, totally cooked in the microwave, rub salt into the skins before cooking.

. . . .

When cooking carrots, peas, beets, or corn, add a small amount of sugar to the water to keep the flavor.

. . . .

Cook root vegetables quickly in 1 inch (5 centimeters) of water in a covered pot. Their taste and color will be better.

. . . .

To peel carrots quickly, immerse in hot water for a few seconds and the skin will scrape off easily.

. . . .

Keep carrots from going soft by cutting a slice off the top and bottom and store them in an airtight container in the refrigerator.

ONIONS & MUSHROOMS

Reduce the time-consuming job of peeling shallots by pouring boiling water over them and leaving for half an hour; the skins will come away easily.

. . . .

To avoid tears when chopping onions, cut them in half with the skin on. Leave them to rest cut-side down for a few minutes to drain out the juice, then peel and chop. Alternatively, before peeling onions, heat them in the microwave for one minute. Or peel onions under a running tap.

. . . .

Get rid of onion smells from your hands by rinsing your hands in water and then rubbing them over stainless steel taps or a sink. Or rinse hands in a little milk before washing as usual.

. . . .

To prevent the smell of cooking onions from spreading around the house, rub a mint leaf around the bottom of the pan you are using. Or keep a damp newspaper nearby when frying onions; it absorbs the smell.

. . . .

For tasty and crisp onion rings, soak them in milk for ten minutes and drain well before frying in hot vegetable oil.

. . . .

When frying onions, add a dash of vinegar or a little sugar and they will brown faster.

. . . .

For crisp fried onions, dip them in egg white or evaporated milk, drain, and coat lightly with flour. Fry quickly in hot fat.

. . . .

When frying onions or other vegetables, if the oil starts to dry up add a drop of water instead of more oil.

. . . .

To quick-fry onions and keep them juicy, put the chopped onions in a pan with a little butter, cover just barely with water, and boil briskly until the water evaporates. Reduce the heat until onions are golden brown.

• • • •

When a recipe calls for finely chopped onion, use a grater instead of a knife to save time.

• • • •

Store mushrooms in a paper bag in the door of the refrigerator, not in the coldest part.

• • • •

Rinse mushrooms in boiling water before frying to stop them shrinking.

SALAD

Place a clean, dry sponge in the vegetable drawer of the refrigerator to absorb moisture; the salad vegetables will keep fresh longer.

• • • •

When washing garden-fresh vegetables for salads or cooking, add a little vinegar to the cold water; any insects will float to the surface.

• • • •

To keep a salad crisp, put an upside down saucer in the bottom of the salad bowl, then add the salad ingredients. Any moisture will collect at the bottom.

· · · ·

Avoid a soggy salad by putting the dressing in the bottom of the salad bowl, cross the salad servers over it, and place the salad on top. Toss the salad just before serving.

· · · ·

Store celery and lettuce in paper bags, not plastic.

· · · ·

To keep celery fresh, trim and wash it. Stand the stalks in a tall jug containing 1 inch (5 centimeters) of water.

· · · ·

Do not remove outer leaves of lettuce until ready to use. Lettuce should be torn into pieces and never cut.

· · · ·

Store tomatoes with stems pointed down and they will stay fresher longer.

· · · ·

Ripen green tomatoes by keeping a ripe tomato or apple with them.

· · · ·

Store tomatoes at room temperature for a couple of hours before serving; it will improve their flavor.

· · · ·

If tomatoes are a little over-ripe, soak them in salted water or ice-cold water for an hour to firm them up.

. . . .

To peel tomatoes easily, place them in a basin, cover with boiling water, remove after half a minute, and plunge into cold water.

. . . .

To keep a cucumber fresh, cut off the end and stand it in half a glass of water in the refrigerator.

OTHER VEGETABLE HINTS

When using canned tomatoes, don't throw away the excess juice. Freeze the juice in an ice cube tray and use for flavoring casseroles or soup at a later date.

. . . .

Add 1 teaspoon (5 milliliters) sugar and a pinch of salt to canned tomatoes when heating them up.

. . . .

When frying tomatoes, dip slices in seasoned flour first and they will not break up. If you are dieting, fry tomatoes in a little tea.

. . . .

Season peas with celery salt instead of ordinary salt.

. . . .

"It's difficult to think anything but pleasant thoughts while eating a homegrown tomato." —Unknown

Cook peas in their pods. When cooked, the pods will open and the peas will float to the top. (The cooking water makes an excellent wine!)

. . . .

Vegetables like snow peas or snap peas should be brought to a boil and then drained and refreshed with cold water so that they retain their bright green color. Reheat with fresh boiling water.

. . . .

To prevent runner beans from becoming limp, store them wrapped in a damp tea-towel in the refrigerator.

. . . .

Use a potato peeler to remove the string from string beans; it's much quicker and safer than with a knife.

. . . .

When cooking corn on the cob, do not add salt to the cooking water or overcook as the corn will become tough.

. . . .

To remove the seeds from a summer squash, cut into slices and use a cookie cutter to lift out the seeds.

. . . .

When boiling beets, leave on all the "whiskers" and a good length of stalk so that it will not bleed during cooking.

. . . .

Use an egg slicer to slice cooked beets for pickling.

• • • •

When pickling beets, boil the vinegar, leave to cool, and add 2 tablespoons (30 milliliters) sweet sherry to the liquid. Interleave the slices with thinly sliced red onion—this removes the earthy flavor.

• • • •

Get avocados or pears to ripen quickly by placing them with a banana in a paper bag. Leave them overnight at room temperature. Or place them in a bowl with apples.

• • • •

To store half an avocado, leave the stone in and smear lemon juice on to the cut surface. Wrap tightly in plastic wrap.

• • • •

To keep the color in guacamole, put some pits back in (until you're ready to eat the guac) and smooth plastic wrap tightly down on the surface to exclude the air.

• • • •

Improve the flavor of frozen or canned spinach by adding 1 tablespoon (15 milliliters) cream, a pinch of salt, freshly grated nutmeg, and black pepper.

• • • •

When cooking fresh spinach, do not add any water; the moisture clinging to the washed leaves will be sufficient for cooking.

• • • •

If vegetables are starting to wrinkle or sprout, peel and dice, then sauté, cool, and freeze. Add stock later to use in soups or stews.

. . . .

To enhance the natural sweetness of carrots or turnips, add a pinch of sugar or orange juice while cooking.

. . . .

To prevent vegetables or fruits going brown after peeling or slicing, drop them in a bowl of water with a squeeze of lemon.

. . . .

Add a small knob of butter to the water of boiling vegetables to stop them boiling over.

. . . .

When draining boiled vegetables at the sink, turn on the cold tap to reduce the steam.

THE SPICE RACK

Allspice—Also known as Jamaica pepper or pimento. These small dark, reddish-brown berries are called allspice because their aroma and flavor resemble a combination of cinnamon, cloves, and nutmeg. Sold whole or ground. They have a strong flavor, so are best combined with other spices in fruitcakes, pies, or pickles. Use whole in marinades.

. . . .

Caraway—Small, brown, crescent-shaped seeds with a strong licorice flavor. Especially delicious as a flavoring in braised cabbage and sauerkraut recipes, breads (particularly rye), cakes, and cheeses.

. . . .

Cardamom—Smallish triangular-shaped pods containing numerous small black seeds which have a warm, highly aromatic, slightly lemony flavor. Used in curries, beef, and pork dishes, Danish pastries, cakes, stewed fruits, and fruit salad. Good in combination with honey.

. . . .

Cayenne Pepper—Obtained from small-fruited varieties of capsicum. Should be a dull red color. This ground pepper is extremely hot and pungent. Use with care. May be used in very small amounts in vegetables, in some salad dressings, and in cheese dishes. Paprika, a milder form of red pepper, is a good substitute.

. . . .

Chili Powder—Made from dried red chilies. This red powder varies in flavor and hotness, from mild to hot. A less fiery type is found in chili seasoning.

• • • •

Cinnamon—Shavings of bark from the cinnamon tree are processed and curled to form cinnamon sticks. Also available in ground form. Spicy, fragrant, and sweet, it is used widely in savory and sweet dishes.

• • • •

Cloves—These dried, unopened flower buds give a warm aroma and pungency to foods, but should be used with care as the flavor can become overpowering. Should be dark brown in color. Available ground or whole. Use ground cloves sparingly in soups, sauces, stewed fruits, and apple pies. Whole cloves are excellent in hot lemon, wine, or whisky drinks.

• • • •

Coriander—Available in seed and ground form. These tiny, pale brown seeds have a delicate orange flavor. An essential spice in curry dishes, but also extremely good in pea or carrot soup, roast pork, casseroles, apple pie, cakes, and cookie recipes.

• • • •

Cumin—Sold in seed or ground down. Cumin has a warm, pungent aromatic flavor and is used extensively to flavor curries and many Middle Eastern and Mexican dishes. Use ground or whole in meat dishes and stuffed vegetables.

• • • •

"Variety's the spice of life, that gives it all its flavor."
—Unknown

Curry Powder—A variety of ground spices combined in proper proportion to give a distinct flavor to savory dishes of meat, poultry, fish, and vegetables.

. . . .

Ginger—Fresh ginger root looks like a knobbly stem. It should be peeled and finely chopped, grated, or sliced before use. Also available in ground form, preserved stem ginger, and as crystallized ginger. Invaluable for adding to many savory and sweet dishes and for baking gingerbread and brandy snaps.

. . . .

Mace & Nutmeg—Both are found on the same plant. The nutmeg is the inner kernel of the fruit. When ripe, the fruit splits open to reveal bright red arils, which lie around the shell of the nutmeg and, once dried, are known as mace blades. The flavor of both spices is very similar—warm, sweet, and aromatic, although nutmeg is more delicate than mace. Both spices are also sold ground. Use with vegetables; sprinkled over egg dishes, milk puddings, and custards; in mulled drinks; or to flavor desserts.

. . . .

Paprika—Comes from a variety of pepper (capsicum) and although similar in color to cayenne, this bright red powder has a milder flavor.

. . . .

Pepper—White pepper comes from ripened berries with the outer husks removed. Black pepper comes from unripened berries that dried until dark greenish-black in color. Black pepper is subtler than white. Use white or black peppercorns in marinades and pickling, or freshly ground as a seasoning. Both are available ground. Green peppercorns are also unripe berries with a mild, light flavor. They are canned in brine, pickled, or freeze-dried in jars.

• • • •

Poppy Seeds—These tiny, slate-blue seeds add a nutty flavor to both sweet and savory dishes. Sprinkle over desserts and breads.

• • • •

Saffron—This spice comes from the stigmas of a species of crocus. It has a distinctive flavor and gives a rich yellow coloring to dishes. It is also the most expensive spice to buy. It's available in small packets or jars (either powdered or in strands, the latter being far superior in flavor). This spice is a must for an authentic paella or Cornish saffron cake. Also an extremely good flavoring for a variety of soups, fish, and chicken dishes.

• • • •

Sesame Seeds—High in protein and mineral oils, sesame seeds have a crisp texture and a sweet, nutty flavor which combines well in curries and with chicken, pork, and fish dishes. Sprinkle over bread, cookies, and pastries before baking.

• • • •

Star Anise—This dried, star-shaped seed head has a pungent, aromatic smell, rather similar to fennel. Use very sparingly in stir-fry dishes. Also good with fish and poultry.

• • • •

Turmeric—Closely related to ginger, turmeric is an aromatic root, which is dried and ground to produce a bright, orange-yellow powder. It has a rich, warm, distinctive smell, a delicate, aromatic flavor, and helps give dishes an attractive yellow coloring. Use in curries, fish, shellfish, rice, and lentil dishes. It is also a necessary ingredient in mustard pickles and piccalilli.

. . . .

When to add spices:
- Casseroles, stews: add at start of cooking.
- Grilled foods: add at the beginning, rubbed into the meat.
- Cakes and pies: add when mixing.
- Uncooked dishes: add well in advance of use to allow flavors to infuse and mellow.

HERBS

Revive herbs by placing the stems in a jar of cold water. Tie a plastic bag over the herbs and leave in a cool place.

. . . .

Freeze chopped fresh parsley in ice cube trays with a little water. When frozen, put into a plastic bag, label, and use when parsley is required for soups, etc.

. . . .

Keep fresh parsley from losing its color in a boiled dish by first pouring boiling water over it to blanch it.

. . . .

"A man taking basil from a woman will love her always."
—Unknown

To have bright, crisp herbs for winter, spread freshly gathered herbs on a piece of paper and place in a cool oven with the door left open. Do not allow them to heat up. When dry, crush the leaves and put in a bottle with a cork stopper. The herbs will retain their green color and fresh taste. Store in a cool dark place.

· · · ·

Tie clean, fresh herbs in small bunches, hang upside down in a warm, dry room or airing cupboard until they are crisp and the leaves crumbly when crushed.

· · · ·

Bay leaves will stay fresher for longer if stored in an airtight jar with a piece of cotton wool dampened with olive oil.

· · · ·

Chervil, dill, chives, basil, parsley, and tarragon all freeze well. For herbs with large leaves, pluck the leaves from the stalks and pack into strong plastic bags, squeezing out as much air as possible. Seal, label, and freeze for up to six months. Chives and herbs with small leaves are best frozen in small bunches. Pack and freeze as before.

· · · ·

To keep mint sauce fresh all year round, drench finely chopped fresh mint in two or three tablespoons of runny honey and store. Simply add vinegar as required.

· · · ·

Prolong the life of fresh supermarket-bought basil by re-potting it immediately into a terracotta pot. Water it frequently and it will last for months and grow back every time you snip a bit off.

THE HERB RACK

Basil—Sometimes called the "tomato herb" because it's delicious with tomato dishes. Used in many Italian dishes. Tear the leaves when sprinkling over dishes. Basil's flavor develops on cooking.

• • • •

Bay Leaves—Particularly good in many meat dishes, as well as in vegetable and meat soups and sauces.

• • • •

Chervil—Looks like parsley but has a smaller leaf and a more aniseed taste.

• • • •

Chives—Long, hollow, grass-like leaves with a mild onion flavor. Snip finely for the best flavor. Used for garnish and good in omelets, scrambled eggs, and salads. The tiny purple flowers can be separated into sprigs by rubbing gently between the fingers, then sprinkled over salads and soups.

• • • •

Coriander—Looks like flat-leaf parsley but lighter in color. Has a sharp, aromatic flavor and distinctive aroma. Used as a garnish and to flavor chutney, vegetable, fish, and meat dishes.

• • • •

Dill—Has a sweet flavor with a delicate taste of aniseed. Good with all fish. Can be chopped into salads, especially cucumber dishes. Add towards the end of cooking.

• • • •

Fennel—Looks like dill but has a sweet aniseed taste that is totally different. Root, stalk, and leaf are used in cooking. Good with fish, or use the raw root in salads.

• • • •

Marjoram—Slightly bitter flavor. Used in onion and mushroom soup, herb bread, and many other dishes.

• • • •

Mint—Tends to go black quickly after chopping, so use immediately. May be used fresh in salads, fruit beverages, jellies, conserves, ices, iced tea, sauces for meats, and added minced to carrots and peas.

• • • •

Oregano—Strong, pleasant, herby flavor. Essential in Italian dishes, especially tomato-based. Gives a boost to boiled cabbage.

• • • •

Parsley—Has tight curly or flat open leaves. The most commonly used herb for garnishing. Use finely chopped and added just before serving to most vegetables and white sauces. May be used in fruit and vegetable salads, in sandwiches, all soups and gravies, as well as meat sauces.

• • • •

Rosemary—Used fresh or dried. Has a strong bittersweet aromatic/spicy taste that needs to be cooked. Particularly good with lamb but can be used with chicken or beef. Add to the dish when roasting vegetables. Use to flavor olive oil.

· · · ·

Rosemary Oil—Add three sprigs of rosemary and 2 teaspoons (10 milliliters) black peppercorns to 1 pint (600 milliliters) light olive oil.

· · · ·

Sage—Fresh or dried, has a strong flavor so use sparingly in poultry and meat stuffing, in sausage and most meat mixtures, in cheese and vegetable combinations, vegetable loaf, patties, etc. The pretty blue flowers are sometimes used in salads.

· · · ·

Sorrel—Looks like a dock leaf and has a sharp lemony flavor. Good in salads. Add to hollandaise sauce to make it green.

· · · ·

Tarragon—Leaves have a hot, pungent taste, so use sparingly. Useful for flavoring salad dressing and sauces, especially tartar sauce. Pickle the leaves with gherkins.

· · · ·

Tarragon Vinegar—Add three sprigs of fresh tarragon to 1 pint (600 milliliters) white wine vinegar or cider vinegar.

· · · ·

Thyme—Small leaves, green or dried, with a fairly strong flavor, so use with care. Good in stuffing, sauces, soups, and meats.

• • • •

Bouquet Garni—Comprises bay leaves, a few sprigs of thyme, parsley stalks, and sometimes a sprig of rosemary or sage, all tied together with cotton thread. Remove from the dish before serving.

When to add herbs:
- In soups and stews: add with the stock.
- In meat loaves, stuffing, etc: add when mixing.
- When roasting: sprinkle on towards the end of cooking.
- Steaks and chops: sprinkle on while cooking.
- Vegetables, sauces or gravy: towards the end of cooking.

THE FRUIT BASKET

To peel apples—pour boiling water over the fruit and leave for a few minutes. Or core the apples, split the skin, and place them in the microwave for two minutes. When cool the skin removes easily.

• • • •

Save apple peelings. To 1 pound (450 grams) of peels, add the grated rind of a lemon, 1 tablespoon (15 milliliters) sugar, and 1 pint (600 milliliters) boiling water. Infuse until cold and serve as a refreshing drink.

• • • •

To prevent peeled apples from going brown, immerse them immediately in moderately salted water or water with a little added lemon juice.

• • • •

When stewing apples, use less sugar and add a teaspoon
of maple syrup.

• • • •

Keep fruit whole when stewing by bringing the water or syrup to
a boil before adding the fruit, then simmer gently until soft.

• • • •

Coat apple rings with egg and breadcrumbs and deep fry or grill.

• • • •

Use leftover apples in your pork stir-fry.

• • • •

For roast pork or chicken, make applesauce with a dash of cider
vinegar plus a few added sultanas.

• • • •

Pack stewed fruit into a freezer bag and then inside a clean milk
carton for easy storing.

• • • •

Chop rhubarb with scissors and the skin will not pull off.
Try sweetening to taste with honey instead of sugar.

• • • •

Add a pinch of ground ginger or grated lemon rind to rhubarb
pie for a lovely flavor.

• • • •

"It is, in my view, the duty of an apple to be crisp and crunchable, but a pear should have such a texture as leads to silent consumption."—Unknown

When making a rhubarb tart, spread the piecrust with blackcurrant or raspberry jam before adding the rhubarb; this helps prevent the piecrust from getting soggy and adds flavor.

• • • •

Add unripe pears or avocado to a dish of apples and they will soon ripen. Or place the unripe fruit and a banana in a paper bag overnight.

• • • •

To ripen green bananas or tomatoes, wrap them in a wet cloth and place in a paper bag.

• • • •

The best flavored bananas are short and thick.

• • • •

To halt the ripening process and stop bananas going brown, try wrapping them individually in aluminum foil, then store in the refrigerator.

• • • •

When preparing a fruit salad a few hours in advance, cover the unpeeled bananas with cold water and leave for 15 minutes. Then peel and add to the fruit salad; this should prevent them from going black.

• • • •

Sprinkle banana slices with lemon juice to prevent
them turning black.

• • • •

Bananas will freeze successfully if you peel and slice them before
placing in an airtight container in the freezer. Or peel them and
wrap in plastic wrap before storing in freezer bags.

• • • •

Ripen hard fruit by placing it in a bowl surrounded by bananas.

• • • •

Eat fresh pineapple as soon as possible after purchase.

• • • •

A pineapple is ripe when the scent comes through the skin but
the leaves are still stiff.

• • • •

Store fresh fruit in a colander; the holes allow the air to circulate
and prevent the fruit from sweating or rotting.

SOFT FRUIT

If freezing blackcurrants, don't bother to top and tail them. When you're ready to use them, just rub them gently between the fingers and the ends will drop off easily.

• • • •

When cooking whole cherries, prick well with a pin before cooking to prevent them from bursting.

• • • •

Wrap strawberries in cabbage leaves before refrigerating to make them last longer.

• • • •

Do not remove strawberry stalks until after washing the fruit.

• • • •

To clean strawberries, soak for a short time in water with 1 teaspoon (5 milliliters) vinegar added. This will remove all small insects. Rinse well.

• • • •

To freeze strawberries or raspberries, rinse in ice cold water and dry thoroughly on a clean cloth, then remove hulls. Open freeze on flat trays, then pack frozen without sugar in zip top plastic bags.

• • • •

To enhance the flavor of strawberries, sprinkle with lemon or orange juice and let stand for 20 minutes before serving. Alternatively, use an orange flavored liqueur.

• • • •

To remove the skin from peaches, grapes, or tomatoes, pop them into a pan of boiling water for two minutes and then into cold water. Use a potato peeler on hard peaches.

. . . .

If you are storing a melon in the refrigerator, make sure to keep it in a sealed plastic bag or it will absorb the flavors of other food. Remove it from the refrigerator 30 minutes before serving.

. . . .

To test melon for ripeness, press the opposite end of the fruit from the stalk with your thumb—if it "gives" a bit, then the fruit is ripe. It should also have a fragrant smell.

CITRUS FRUITS

Citrus fruit should always feel heavy for their size.

. . . .

Lemons warmed before use will give double the juice.

. . . .

Store lemons in a covered plastic box in the refrigerator and they will keep fresh for weeks.

. . . .

To keep half a lemon: sprinkle the cut side with sugar and place on a saucer. This will keep for a few days in the refrigerator.

. . . .

"It is probable that the lemon is the most valuable of all fruit for preserving health."—Unknown

If you only need the rind of an orange or lemon: squeeze the juice into an ice cube tray and freeze for future use.

• • • •

When only the juice is required, store the skins in the freezer. They will easily grate from frozen when needed.

• • • •

When only a few slices of lemon or lime are needed, slice the remainder and open freeze till solid. Place in a zip top plastic bag and use for drinks as required.

• • • •

Fresh fruit will last longer if a fresh lemon is kept in the fruit bowl.

• • • •

Before grating lemons, run the grater under cold water and the gratings will slip off easily.

• • • •

Finely grate the rinds of oranges and lemons, add an equal amount of superfine sugar, store in a screw-top jar, and use to flavor cakes and puddings.

. . . .

Grated lemon or orange peel can be added to icing sugar and used to flavor butter or glace icing, with the addition of a few drops of fresh orange or lemon juice.

. . . .

Soak oranges in boiling water for five minutes before peeling and the white pithy part should peel off easily. Or put in the microwave for 20–30 seconds.

. . . .

To make orange segments, peel the orange and remove all the pith. Hold the orange in the left hand over a dish or plate and, with a sharp knife, dissect out each segment, leaving the membrane behind.

. . . .

When cutting grapefruit segments, use a cheese knife as its curved end will make the job easier.

PRESERVES

To sterilize jars, wash in warm, soapy water, then rinse thoroughly in warm water. Dry well with a clean towel. Place upside down in a moderate oven for five to ten minutes. Use warm or cold.

. . . .

When making jam, choose a good quality, large saucepan with a heavy base. To allow room for the jam to boil vigorously, the pan should be about half full when the sugar has been added. Remove the scum at the end of cooking.

• • • •

Grease the inside of the cooking pan with butter to prevent the jam burning or boiling over. It also reduces scum and makes it easier to clean.

• • • •

Jam is best made from slightly under-ripe fruit. Sufficient sugar must be added. The general rule is to use 1 pound (450 grams) sugar to 1 pound unripe fruit and ¾ pound (350 grams) sugar to 1 pound ripe fruit.

• • • •

Put the pits from stone fruit (such as plums) in muslin and cook in the jam to improve the flavor.

• • • •

For jam making, use granulated sugar. Castor sugar or brown sugar produce a lot of froth and are not recommended.

• • • •

Warm the sugar for making jam in a heatproof bowl in the oven at 300°F while you are cooking the fruit. It will dissolve more quickly.

• • • •

The fruit should be cooked until soft to extract all the pectin before adding the sugar.

• • • •

After adding the warm sugar, allow it time to dissolve completely before boiling the jam rapidly to reach setting point. Do not over-stir jam.

. . . .

Never fill a jam kettle or saucepan more than half full as the jam may boil over.

. . . .

Clip a clothes peg onto the handle of the wooden spoon and place it over the edge of the pan to prevent the spoon falling in.

. . . .

Stir in a figure eight pattern to keep the jam from sticking to the pan.

. . . .

Over-boiled jam will be dark colored and sugary.

. . . .

A sugar thermometer will register about 220°F/105°C once setting point has been reached.

. . . .

To test if jam is at setting point, remove the saucepan from the heat and drop a teaspoonful of jam onto an ice-cold plate. After a minute, the surface should set and crinkle when pushed with a finger.

. . . .

If jam will not set, re-boil it with 2 tablespoons (30 milliliters) of fresh lemon juice or the recommended amount of pectin to each 4 pounds (1.8 kilograms) of fruit.

. . . .

To thicken watery jam, soak seed pearl tapioca in water—½ ounce (12 grams) for each 1 pound (450 grams) of jam—for 12 hours, add to the jam, and bring to a boil and boil until clear. This jam will not store well so it should be used quickly.

. . . .

To thin jam, return jam to the pan and add some water, then re-boil and re-can.

. . . .

When canning jam, sterilize screw-top jars, fill each warmed jar to the top with hot jam, cover immediately with a circle of waxed paper, and screw on lids or use transparent covers secured tightly with a rubber band. Turn the jars upside down until cold.

. . . .

Store jars of jam right way up in a dry airy cupboard. Do not leave on a high kitchen shelf as the rising heat may cause it to ferment.

. . . .

To restore slightly fermented jam, remove the surface of the jam and put the remainder into a saucepan and boil for 20 minutes. If it is badly fermented it is unusable.

. . . .

If homemade jam becomes sugary, stand the jar in a saucepan of cold water and heat slowly until the sugar dissolves.

. . . .

When making jelly from fruit, allow 1 pound (450 grams) of sugar to every 1 pint (600 milliliters) of juice. Do not overboil. Test, bottle, and store as for jam.

. . . .

When making marmalade, add a pint of pineapple juice instead of water for a delicious flavor.

. . . .

For a darker colored marmalade with a richer taste, use half demerara sugar when cooking.

. . . .

Marmalade will be much clearer if, half way through cooking, you add 2 teaspoons (10 milliliters) glycerine for every 8 pounds (4 kilograms) of jam.

. . . .

Cover jars of chutney with clear plastic film before putting on a metal lid. This prevents the metal from reacting with the acid in the chutney and causing deterioration.

. . . .

Chutney is ready when the vinegar has reduced sufficiently. Make a channel across the surface with a wooden spoon. If the indentation is not filled with vinegar for a few seconds then the chutney is ready.

. . . .

All chutneys should be stored in a cool dark place for at least three months before using to let them mature and mellow in flavor.

. . . .

When labeling jars of homemade preserves, use masking tape as it peels off easily and doesn't leave a sticky residue.

DRIED FRUIT & NUTS

Do not store dried fruit in tins as the acid content of the fruit can cause the tin to corrode.

. . . .

Candied peel must be moist and clear. If dull and cloudy it is not fresh and will lack flavor.

. . . .

No need to wash good quality dried fruit; just rub with a dry towel.

. . . .

Before using sticky fruit such as raisins or dates, warm them in the oven and they will separate easily.

. . . .

Use a wet knife to chop dried fruit and it will not stick to the blade. Use scissors instead of a knife to chop dates or dried apricots.

. . . .

Use warm—not boiling—water to soften dried apricots or prunes to avoid the skin becoming hard.

. . . .

For delicious prunes, soak them in cold tea overnight and stew in the same liquid until tender.

. . . .

Put dates through a mincer before making a date loaf.

. . . .

To skin hazelnuts, toast the nuts until lightly colored, put them into a paper bag, and rub between your hands. This should remove the skins.

. . . .

To shell walnuts without breaking, soak them overnight in salted water. Squeeze gently with nutcrackers.

. . . .

Warm nuts for 30 minutes in a low oven or soak in cold salted water overnight—crack carefully and the kernels will stay whole.

. . . .

To blanch almonds, place whole almonds in a basin and pour boiling water over them. Leave for five minutes. Drain. The skin will come off easily by pinching between the finger and thumb.

Household Chores

KITCHEN TIPS

To keep your house insect free, spray around doors and windows with a water and tea tree oil mixture.

. . . .

When you have a large number of guests and no room to heat plates in the oven, put them in the dishwasher and run it on a dry cycle to warm the plates.

. . . .

Heat plates quickly by putting them into hot water and then dry just before use. Or place 1 tablespoon (15 milliliters) water on each plate and stack them in the microwave. Heat for one minute each on High.

. . . .

Instead of using freezer packs, freeze small bottles of water and pack them in the cooler. They keep the food chilled and provide a cool drink.

. . . .

Used herb or spice jars are useful containers for salad dressing or other condiments when going on a picnic.

. . . .

Put crumpled paper towel inside washed and dried twist-top jam jars when storing them. It absorbs any moisture and stops the lids from corroding.

. . . .

Make a hand-revolving shelf for spice jars and sauces. Put a screw through the center of a round metal tin tray or lid and screw it onto a shelf so it can be turned easily.

• • • •

Place a layer of tinfoil between a casserole lid and the dish; the contents will not boil over and the lid will be easily cleaned.

• • • •

Use the back of a wooden spoon to spread butter or margarine on tinfoil and it will not tear the sheet.

• • • •

Twist a piece of tinfoil into a cone to make a strong icing bag.

POTS & PANS

To clean a burnt pan, put half a cup of baking soda in the pan and fill it half full with water. Bring to a boil and simmer until the particles float to the top.

• • • •

To help clean the saucepan after scrambled egg: immediately after use hold the pan upside down under a cold running tap for a few minutes.

• • • •

"The way to get things done is not to mind who gets the credit for doing them."—Benjamin Jowett

Milk saucepans are easier to clean if they are immediately turned upside down after use and left to stand for a few minutes before washing.

. . . .

Used tinfoil screwed up in a ball is excellent for removing the initial mess from burnt saucepans.

. . . .

Invert a burnt pan over another pan of boiling water and the steam will help to remove the burnt food.

. . . .

To clean a burnt aluminum saucepan, pour water into the pot and add an onion. Bring to a boil and the burnt matter will loosen and rise to the top, leaving the saucepan bright and clean.

. . . .

Remove discoloration from an aluminum saucepan by filling it with a solution of 1 tablespoon (15 milliliters) vinegar and 2 pints (1.2 liters) water. Heat slowly and boil for five minutes. Rinse well with clean cold water. Dry thoroughly before storing. Avoid using washing soda or alkaline water when washing aluminum.

. . . .

To clean copper pots, fill a 1 pint (600 milliliters) spray bottle with vinegar and 3 tablespoons (45 milliliters) of salt. Spray on the copper, let stand for an hour, then rub clean.

. . . .

Remove stains on copper pans by sprinkling them with salt and scouring with a cloth soaked in vinegar.

. . . .

To clean a saucepan after making caramel/toffee, fill it with warm water and bring it to a boil.

. . . .

To keep the metal grill of a barbecue clean, rub it over with a raw potato before each use.

. . . .

Clean a badly encrusted barbecue grill by soaking it in leftover brewed coffee. Scrub well and wash as usual.

. . . .

Lay a barbecue grill rack on the lawn overnight; the dew will combine with the enzymes in the grass to loosen any burned-on grease. Try this with dirty oven racks too.

. . . .

New cake pans should be greased inside and outside with lard and placed in a hot oven until they are very hot. Remove the tins, cool, and wash in warm soapy water.

. . . .

Baking pans are less likely to rust if, after washing, they are dried thoroughly in the oven while it's cooling down.

. . . .

When lining a cake pan with greaseproof paper, dab a little margarine on the side of the pan so that the paper will stick to it and not move around when adding the mixture.

· · · ·

Before using glass or earthenware casserole dishes, rub the outside with a raw onion to prevent the dish cracking while being heated.

· · · ·

To cut through grease on pans, rub over with a used tea bag before washing.

· · · ·

A pinch of salt added to the frying pan when melting butter or oil will prevent it spitting.

· · · ·

If your frying pan is sticking, brush with a small amount of oil, sprinkle with 3 tablespoons (45 milliliters) salt, and heat gently for three minutes. Rub the salt around the pan with paper towel, then wipe off with a dry cloth.

· · · ·

Soak discolored oven dishes overnight in a solution of hot water with 2 tablespoons (30 milliliters) baking soda added. Or soak overnight in warm water with ¼ pint (150 milliliters) bleach to 4 pints (2.5 liters) of water. Rinse well.

. . . .

To remove stubborn food deposits from casserole dishes, fill with boiling water, add 3 tablespoons (45 milliliters) baking soda or salt, and leave for an hour.

CLEANING UTENSILS

Remove metal abrasion marks from the glazed coating of cups by rubbing with toothpaste and rinsing well.

. . . .

To remove tea stains from china cups, rub with a slice of lemon, then rinse. Alternatively, add boiling water to 2 teaspoons (10 milliliters) baking soda, leave the cups to soak for 30 minutes, and rinse well.

. . . .

Keep a small hard toothbrush beside the sink for cleaning inaccessible crevices in wire whisks or graters.

. . . .

To clean discolored wooden spoons, soak them overnight in 1 pint (600 milliliters) hot water with 2 tablespoons (30 milliliters) lemon juice.

. . . .

Brighten a dull kitchen floor after mopping by wiping it over with a solution of 1 cup (250 milliliters) white vinegar in a bucket of water.

• • • •

To clean coffee pots, fill with water, add 4 tablespoons (60 milliliters) of salt to the water, and percolate or boil as usual.

• • • •

To remove tannin staining from inside the teapot, fill with a solution of water and biological washing powder and leave for a few hours. Rinse thoroughly before use.

• • • •

To collect calcium deposits in a kettle, cut off a small piece of loofah and place it inside the kettle. Use as normal. When it gets encrusted, remove the loofah and rinse well before returning to the kettle.

• • • •

To remove scale from an electric kettle, cover the element with equal parts of vinegar and water. Bring to a boil, then leave the water in overnight. Next morning, rinse well with cold water. Boil and discard a kettleful of water before use.

KITCHEN STAINS & ODORS

When a pan smells of fish, soak in tea for ten minutes before washing, or add vinegar to the dish water. Or pour cold water into the frying pan, add some baking soda, and bring to a boil.

• • • •

Remove food coloring stains from your skin or work surface by rubbing with a piece of raw potato.

. . . .

To clean yellowing ovenproof dishes, soak overnight in 4 pints (2 liters) warm water with an added cup (250 milliliters) of bleach. Rinse thoroughly before using.

. . . .

Rub the inside of plastic containers with vegetable oil before adding tomato-based food, to prevent staining.

. . . .

A few drops of vanilla essence in water will remove smells from plastic containers.

. . . .

For stains on a laminated worktop, apply a paste of baking soda and water with a cloth. Rub off after a few minutes.

. . . .

To remove a musty smell from a cupboard or wardrobe, empty it and place a cup of just-boiled milk inside and close the doors. Leave for a few hours.

• • • •

To remove a musty smell from a plastic container, wash and dry it and then place in the freezer for 48 hours. The lingering smell should disappear. Or put a piece of white bread soaked in white vinegar in the container and leave closed overnight.

• • • •

To remove the smell of garlic from hands, rub them over any stainless steel appliance.

• • • •

To remove onion odors from hands, rub fingers with salt before washing.

• • • •

To remove odors in a dishwasher, sprinkle baking soda in the bottom and leave overnight. Any spots can be removed with a damp cloth dipped in baking soda.

• • • •

Remove an unpleasant lingering smell from the kitchen by placing a few vanilla pods in an open jar. Or try baking some orange peel in a moderate oven for 15 minutes.

KITCHEN APPLIANCES

Remove any grease splatters or dried food from stovetops
or counters by rubbing with baking soda on a damp sponge.
Wipe with a clean damp cloth.

. . . .

Scrape off burnt-on food stains on the glass door of an oven with
a disposable razor before cleaning as usual.

. . . .

To remove marks from stainless steel appliances,
polish with baby oil.

. . . .

If food is spilled in the oven while cooking, sprinkle with salt and
when the oven cools it will be easy to wipe off. Or cover the spill
with automatic dishwashing powder, cover with wet paper towel,
and leave for a few hours. Clean with a damp cloth.

. . . .

Cover burnt spillage in the oven with tomato paste. Leave
overnight and then wipe off with a soft cloth and warm soapy
water.

. . . .

After using the oven for greasy cooking, place a bowl of ammonia
on the bottom rack while the oven is still warm. Leave overnight,
then the oven can be easily cleaned.

. . . .

After cleaning the oven, rub a solution of 1 tablespoon (15 milliliters) baking soda to ½ pint (300 milliliters) water over the surface and it will be easier to clean next time.

. . . .

To remove the smell of solvents from a recently cleaned oven, heat some lemon rind in a 350°F oven for 15 minutes. Open the oven door and cook for another ten minutes.

. . . .

A mixture of salt and a pinch of cinnamon sprinkled on a hot oven or stove burner will remove the "burnt food" odor. When dry, remove the salted spots with a stiff brush or cloth.

. . . .

Toss salt on a grease fire on the stove or in the oven and it will smother the flames. Never use water; it will only make the hot grease spatter.

. . . .

To remove traces of tea, coffee, or hard water deposits from a sink, cut a lemon in half, rub over the surface, and squeeze the juice around the drain. Leave overnight and rinse in the morning.

. . . .

For a gleaming stainless steel sink, sprinkle a little flour on a dry sink, then buff with a duster.

. . . .

For a shiny white sink, cover with paper towels saturated in bleach. Leave to stand for 30 minutes, then rinse thoroughly with cool water.

. . . .

For clogged drains, pour ½ cup (125 milliliters) of baking soda over the drain, and then pour 1 cup (250 milliliters) of vinegar over it. Leave for a minute until it foams, then pour boiling water down the drain. Sometimes difficult blockages will need the process repeated.

. . . .

To dissolve grease in a clogged drain, pour 1 cup (250 milliliters) baking soda and 1 cup of salt down the drain followed by a large amount of boiling water.

. . . .

To stop sinks and drainpipes giving off unpleasant smells, sprinkle 1 tablespoon (15 milliliters) of freshly ground coffee down the drain and rinse with plenty of water.

. . . .

Rub kitchen tiles with scrunched up newspaper to keep them free of grease.

. . . .

Run vinegar through the dishwasher once a month to prevent hard deposits forming in it.

. . . .

When a refrigerator magnet keep slipping,
place a piece of tissue behind it.

. . . .

If you need to turn off the refrigerator for a long period, empty
of all food items, wash down, and place a saucer with 1 teaspoon
(5 milliliters) coffee granules in it to prevent unpleasant odors
from forming.

. . . .

Stop ice cube trays from sticking in the freezer by smearing the
bottom of the tray with glycerine.

. . . .

When cleaning the refrigerator, add a few drops of vanilla extract
to the water to keep it fresh.

. . . .

To eliminate smelly odors, keep an open box of baking soda or a
piece of cotton dipped in vanilla extract in your refrigerator.

. . . .

Prevent mildew by wiping down the inside of the refrigerator
occasionally with white vinegar.

. . . .

Salt and soda water will clean and sweeten the inside of your
refrigerator. It will not scratch enamel either.

. . . .

To clean underneath the fridge, tie a sock around
the end of a broom handle.

. . . .

If you need to pull out your oven, freezer, or dishwasher to clean
behind them, sprinkle some talcum powder on the floor in front
of them and they will slide out easily.

. . . .

To defrost the freezer quickly, remove the food and wrap in a
blanket or in plenty of newspapers to keep frozen. Switch off the
power, put some newspapers in the bottom of the freezer, and
place a large pan of boiling water inside the freezer. Close the
lid or door and leave for 20–30 minutes. Using a broad plastic
spatula, the ice will scrape off easily. Wipe down the sides and
bottom with clean water. Put some glycerine on a clean cloth and
rub around the sides of the freezer to ensure the easy removal of
ice the next time you are defrosting. Switch on the freezer, return
the food, and turn on the boost switch for half an hour.

KITCHEN EQUIPMENT

Before using new china, put it in a large saucepan lined with a cloth and cover with cold water. Bring slowly to a boil, turn off the heat, and allow to cool in the water.

. . . .

If you keep silver cutlery in a drawer, line it with blotting paper to avoid it becoming tarnished.

. . . .

Always keep kitchen graters and pastry cutters in a warm place to dry off after washing. This prevents them from becoming rusty.

. . . .

Wipe the inside of a bread bin with a cloth sprinkled with vinegar for extra freshness.

. . . .

After washing with soap and water, rub cutting boards with a damp cloth dipped in salt.

. . . .

To clean cotton dishcloths quickly, place them in a large glass bowl with 1 tablespoon (15 milliliters) of baking soda, cover with water, and microwave for three minutes.

. . . .

When using a mixing bowl, keep it from slipping by putting a damp cloth underneath.

. . . .

"Housework is something you do that no one notices until you don't."
—Unknown

To sharpen a pair of scissors, cut into a piece of tin foil folded in four a few times.

• • • •

Sharpen a blunt potato peeler by inserting an old nail file into the slot and rubbing the edge of the cutter firmly.

• • • •

Wooden salad bowls should be rubbed with pure corn oil to prevent the wood being damaged by vinegar or water.

• • • •

If a bread wrapper or plastic bag melts on the surface of a hot toaster, rub the area with nail polish remover.

When hot fat is spilled on a floor or wooden surface, pour cold water on it immediately. This will solidify the fat so it can be easily scraped off. Wash the area afterwards with hot soapy water.

HANDY HINTS

Keep margarine wrappers stored in the refrigerator for greasing baking pans.

• • • •

To loosen screw-top jars or bottles, tap the center of the lid and the edges will expand.

• • • •

Before washing crystal or fine china, put a towel in the sink
to cushion the pieces.

• • • •

When two glasses are stuck together, fill the top one with cold
water and dip the bottom one in hot water.

• • • •

Scratches on glassware will disappear if you polish them
with toothpaste.

• • • •

To clean a blender, fill the container halfway up with hot water
plus a couple of drops of dishwasher detergent. Cover and blend,
rinse and dry.

• • • •

To prevent rusting soap pads, wrap the pads in tinfoil and keep
them immersed in a small pot of water or sprinkle a little baking
soda in the bottom of the dish in which you leave them.

• • • •

Aluminum foil makes a sensible cover
for a regularly used recipe book.

• • • •

Plastic wrap kept in the refrigerator is much easier to handle.

• • • •

Heavy books stored on a shelf should be turned upside down every
few months to prevent the pages sagging and the binding splitting.

• • • •

If your books smell a little musty, place the book in a plastic bag with some baking soda. Shake and leave the book in the bag overnight. Remove book and wipe off soda.

PEST CONTROL

To get rid of ants, mix borax powder or talcum powder with sugar and leave near the nest. They will eat it and take it back to the nest and eradicate the queen ant. But keep out of reach of young children and pets.

• • • •

Rather than putting cheese in a mousetrap, consider peanut butter, bacon, nuts, or chocolate. Mice seem to prefer them.

• • • •

Cockroaches like damp areas, so seal up cracks and replace any damp, decaying wood. Keep shelves and pipes dry and clean. Sprinkle borax freely wherever you see signs of entry. Replace the borax frequently.

• • • •

To avoid clothes moths, make sure that clothes are clean. Brush and hang all woolen clothing, blankets, or furs in the sun and check for moths or larvae before storing. If there are larvae on stored articles they will hatch and ruin the material. Store in sealed boxes or moth-proof bags. Or wrap in newspaper and store in a tightly closed cotton bag. Camphor, cedar, or moth balls do not kill larvae, but they will deter the moths.

• • • •

"There is nothing so easy to learn as experience and nothing so hard to apply." —Unknown

To discourage house spiders, soak cotton balls in pennyroyal oil and place the cotton balls around where the spiders live.

• • • •

If mosquitoes are prevalent around your home, remove all puddles of water, as this is where they breed. Cover all outside water containers. Put screens on all doors and windows and rub citronella or cedar oil over the screens to repel mosquitoes.

• • • •

When gardening, burning incense helps to keep mosquitoes away from you. Place four sticks around where you are working.

• • • •

If you are troubled with silverfish, try placing whole cloves in the closets and drawers.

• • • •

To discourage silverfish from books, wipe the shelves with a solution of borax and water. When the shelves are dry, sprinkle a little borax on the back of the shelves before returning the books.

BATHROOM

To wash a shower curtain, fill the washing machine with warm water and two large bath towels. Add ½ cup (125 milliliters) each of detergent and baking soda. Then wash, adding 1 cup (250 milliliters) white vinegar to the rinse cycle. Do not spin dry or wash vinegar out. Hang immediately and the wrinkles will disappear when completely dry.

• • • •

To prevent mildew from forming on a new shower curtain, soak in salted water before hanging for the first time.

• • • •

A good cleaner for shower doors is WD40 spray lubricant.

• • • •

Apply baby oil over your shower doors and tile surface. This prevents scum build-up from dirt and soap.

• • • •

To remove toilet rings, flush to wet the sides and apply a paste of borax and lemon juice. Leave for two hours, then scrub.

• • • •

Toilet bowls come up shiny when cleaned with old, flat cola drinks. Leave overnight to dissolve the limescale.

• • • •

To remove hairspray film from mirrors, carefully wipe with alcohol.

• • • •

"Life is like a mirror. We get the best results when we smile at it."—Unknown

To whiten a bathtub, clean with turpentine and a tablespoon of salt.

· · · ·

Cleaning bathroom mirrors with shampoo will help prevent them from steaming up.

· · · ·

Rub the bathroom mirror with dry soap and then polish with a soft cloth; this will prevent it from steaming up.

· · · ·

To create a fresh, clean aroma in the bathroom, toss a sheet of fabric softener in the wastebasket. Or dab a bit of perfume on a light bulb—the room will be flooded with scent when the light is turned on.

· · · ·

To whiten the grouting between tiles, use white shoe polish, applied with an old toothbrush. Wipe over with a clean, damp cloth.

· · · ·

To remove hard water stains from tiles, apply vinegar and leave for ten minutes before rinsing clean.

· · · ·

Sprinkle a little boric acid on bathroom tiles before washing for economical as well as sparkling results.

· · · ·

When bathroom grout goes gray, touch it up with canvas shoe whitener. Run the sponge applicator down the lines, leave for five minutes, and rub off the excess.

• • • •

A lump of Blu Tack makes a perfect emergency bath or sink plug.

• • • •

If you lose the top of the tube of toothpaste, store it head down in a glass of water to prevent the paste going hard.

• • • •

An upright kitchen roll holder is ideal for storing spare toilet rolls.

• • • •

When the nozzle on an aerosol can becomes clogged, remove the nozzle and place it in a pan of boiling water for a second or two. Leave to dry and replace on can.

• • • •

Cut a small hole in the side of a sponge and slip in any leftover pieces of soap. Use the soapy sponge in the bath.

• • • •

Soak hairbrushes in warm water and shampoo for half an hour and the hair will come away easily.

• • • •

Store a spiky hairbrush in a fabric glasses case so that it doesn't snag the lining of your handbag.

HANDY HINTS

If sunglass lenses or the face of your wristwatch are scratched, rub them gently with a little liquid metal polish on a soft cloth. The scratches will smooth away.

• • • •

Pick up fluff from suede by rubbing it with velvet.

• • • •

When mailing a small fragile present, wrap the object in plenty of well-soaked newspaper, leave to dry, and the paper will have formed a tough protective shell. Or inflate two ice cube bags and wrap them around the article before placing in an envelope.

• • • •

To separate stuck stamps, put them in the freezer for a short time.

• • • •

Spray a dry umbrella on both sides with hairspray to make it water resistant.

• • • •

When drying a wet umbrella, leave it half open so that the material does not stretch and become detached from the spokes.

. . . .

If a collapsible umbrella won't collapse, run a candle up and down the shaft a few times.

. . . .

Before having your photo taken in a booth, sit with your head between your legs for a few seconds. The rush of blood will add color to your cheeks.

. . . .

Before traveling abroad, photocopy your passport and any relevant documents and pack them separately. If your passport is lost, you will have all the information you need.

. . . .

When unpacking after vacations, make a list of all the things you took and did not use, and the things you wish you had taken. Keep the lists in the suitcase for more efficient packing next time.

. . . .

If you need to remember something for the next day, put a note in the shoes you'll be wearing.

. . . .

Fit the rubber end of a walking stick over the head of a Yale lock to make it easier to turn.

. . . .

To speed up the drying of a wet coat, hang it on a coat hanger with a hot-water bottle suspended inside. The gentle heat speeds up the drying process without damaging the coat.

Use a wire suede brush to remove the fluff from Velcro fastenings on clothes or shoes.

· · · ·

To stop CDs from skipping, add some soap to a wet cloth and wipe the CD from the middle outwards. Dry with a soft lintless cloth. If a CD is scratched, put a small amount of toothpaste on a dry cloth and wipe the length of the scratch.

· · · ·

Use a drop of vinegar to thin down thickened glue.

· · · ·

Unroll a packet of cotton and leave in a warm place; it will fluff out to double its size.

· · · ·

Rub sticky playing cards with a slice of white bread.

· · · ·

To frame a large picture cheaply, try your local charity shops as they often stock large framed pictures. Discard the picture and use the frame.

· · · ·

Preserve a child's painting with a coat of hair spray.

· · · ·

When discarding worn out shirts or cardigans, snip off the buttons and attach them to a strip of adhesive tape. This will keep them in their sets for future use.

. . . .

If a newly cut key sticks in the lock, rub the teeth with pencil lead.

. . . .

To dust fabric lampshades, rub them with a piece of white bread, then dust as usual.

. . . .

Clean a door mat without creating dust by putting it in a large trash bag before shaking vigorously.

HELPFUL HINTS

Put the contents of vacuum cleaner bags on the compost heap.

. . . .

Before putting on rubber gloves, drip a drop of olive oil into each finger and it will make the gloves last longer. The oil is also good for your skin.

. . . .

Rubber gloves are difficult to remove if you have been using them in hot water; let the cold tap run over them and they will come off easily.

. . . .

To prevent garbage from getting stuck at the bottom of a large trashcan, make a pad to fit the bottom with folded newspapers wrapped up tightly in a plastic bag. The weight of the pad will push out all the rubbish when it is tipped over.

• • • •

To keep your trashcan from blowing over, attach it to your fence with hooked luggage straps.

• • • •

Get rid of cigarette smells by placing a cup of dry coffee granules in the room; they help to absorb the smell. Or leave a saucerful of vinegar in the room overnight.

• • • •

Remove marks and smells from dirty ashtrays by wiping with a dry, used teabag. Put a thin coat of floor wax on ashtrays and they will be easily wiped clean.

• • • •

A teaspoon in the glass will prevent it cracking when boiling water is poured in.

• • • •

When sewing tough material or carpet, rub the area to be stitched with a candle.

• • • •

Put potpourri into the foot of a pair of tights or socks, tie into a knot, and place behind a radiator. The heat brings out the fragrance.

• • • •

If an electric plug fits too tight and is difficult to pull out, rub its prongs with a soft lead pencil.

• • • •

To remove a tight ring, place the finger in cold water for five minutes. Remove from the water and pour some warm butter around the ring, pull gently off. Or use liquid dish soap as a lubricant to remove stuck rings.

HEAT & LIGHT

Soak candle wicks in vinegar and allow to dry before use; they will give a clearer, brighter light.

• • • •

To avoid candle wax stains, buy good quality candles made from paraffin wax, scent, coloring, and stearic acid which helps the candle burn well, thus reducing dripping. Cheap candles have lots of additives and cause more staining as a result.

• • • •

"Burning the candle at both ends will soon leave you without a light." —Unknown

When using candles, always make sure that they are placed away from drafts. The candleholder should be large enough to catch any drips. Always use a snuffer (or improvise with a small glass) to extinguish candles. Let the wax solidify before moving the candle.

. . . .

To remove a melted candle or clean a candleholder, especially a glass one, place it in the deep freezer for one hour. The wax will chip off more easily.

. . . .

If candle wax drips on a polished wood surface, melt the wax gently with a hair dryer, wipe off the wax with a paper towel, then rub with a little vinegar in warm water. Dry and polish as usual.

. . . .

To prevent water in a floating candle bowl from becoming cloudy, add a drop of baby bottle sterilizing liquid and it will remain clear for weeks.

. . . .

Keep all potato peelings and dry them in the oven when baking. Store in paper bags and use in place of kindling when lighting the fire.

. . . .

A pinch of dried rosemary or lavender sprinkled on embers will scent a room.

. . . .

To make coal last longer and burn brighter, sprinkle with a solution made from 2 tablespoons (30 milliliters) baking soda to 2 pints (1.25 liters) water. Let the coal dry before using.

. . . .

To reduce soot in the chimney, put a handful of salt on a bright fire at least once a week.

CHILDREN & PETS

Use a soft cosmetic brush to remove sand from children's faces at the beach. Tell them to close their eyes and brush downwards.

. . . .

Rub a raw potato on the soles of children's new shoes to prevent them slipping.

. . . .

To remove tar from a child's skin, rub with a mixture of baby oil and dish soap, or rub with a piece of fresh orange peel, then wash in soapy water.

. . . .

Don't throw out shoulder pads; sew them into the knees of children's pants to prevent wear.

. . . .

To stop a child's duvet slipping off the bed, sew a strip of material along the bottom to tuck under the mattress.

. . . .

"The reason a dog has so many friends is that his tail wags instead of his tongue." —Unknown

To stop small children from opening cupboard doors, put a strong elastic band around two adjacent door handles.

. . . .

A lump of margarine fed to a dog three times a week will keep his coat free from dandruff and prevent dry skin. A raw egg given occasionally helps to keep worms at bay.

. . . .

Keep cats or dogs free of fleas by mashing a clove of garlic into his or her food once a week.

. . . .

If cats use the garden as a litter box, remove the mess, then sprinkle diluted vinegar around the area to deter them.

. . . .

To give a cat a pill, place one hand over the cat's head so that your thumb and index finger are just behind the canine teeth. Tip the head back so that its nose tilts upwards and press gently. The mouth should open. Place the tablet as far back in the throat as possible. Close the cat's mouth and gently rub the throat or blow on the nose to stimulate swallowing.

CARS & BIKES

Put baking soda in the car ashtray to reduce odor and quickly extinguish cigarettes.

. . . .

Avoid having a foggy windshield by using a chalkboard eraser instead of a cloth to clean it

. . . .

For a gleaming car windshield, wipe with a sponge dampened with cola. Or add 1 teaspoon (5 milliliters) vinegar to the windshield washer container.

. . . .

To remove stubborn insect marks from a windshield, rub with baking soda on a damp cloth.

. . . .

Keep car headlights free from mud by wiping them over once a week with a cut lemon.

. . . .

For a glittering finish to a newly waxed car, spray with cold water and gently wipe dry.

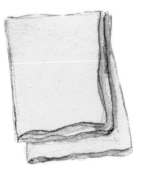

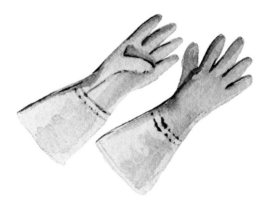

Laundry and Stain Removal

TREATING FABRIC STAINS

Try to treat stains immediately. If you have no available removal remedy, soak the article in cold water.

. . . .

If this does not work, try lukewarm water with ordinary soap or scented soap. Dampen the fabric and rub with soap until the stain is erased. Rinse with lukewarm water, put between two towels, and pat until damp dry. Do not use hot water as this can set the stain.

. . . .

If the stained material is colored, always test the removal remedy on an inconspicuous area first. After applying the removal remedy, rinse the fabric thoroughly in plenty of lukewarm water. Then wash as usual.

. . . .

If using a chemical substance to remove stains, always use a weak solution several times, rather than a strong solution once.

. . . .

When working on a stain, always work in towards the center as working outwards will spread the damage.

. . . .

To avoid watermarks, place the wet article on a towel and press another towel on top.

. . . .

To whiten polyester garments, soak overnight in 1 gallon (3.8 liters) water with an added cup (250 milliliters) of dishwasher detergent. Next day wash as usual.

• • • •

To whiten nylon garments, mix 1 gallon (3.8 liters) of hot water with 6 tablespoons (90 milliliters) dishwasher detergent and 3 tablespoons (45 milliliters) household bleach. Cool to tepid and soak the garments for 30 minutes. Rinse in cool water with a dash of white vinegar added.

• • • •

To whiten woolen garments that have yellowed, mix one part hydrogen peroxide with eight parts water and soak the garment in this for 12 hours.

• • • •

Yellowed cottons or linens can be brightened by boiling the items for one hour in 1 gallon (3.8 liters) of water with 1 tablespoon (15 milliliters) each of salt and baking soda added.

• • • •

Whites that have yellowed from over-bleaching can be restored by soaking in warm water with 2 tablespoons (30 milliliters) malt vinegar added.

LAUNDRY STAINS

Wine stains—apply table salt to a wet wine stain immediately. Allow the salt to absorb the wine. Rinse off with cool water. Reapply if necessary.

. . . .

Beer stains—immediately sponge with a mild vinegar solution. Rinse with lukewarm water, apply a paste of wet biological washing powder, leave for 30 minutes.

. . . .

Old beer stains can be difficult to remove. Soak the garment in cold water overnight and proceed as above.

. . . .

Remove ink stains from washable clothes by spraying with hairspray or perfume, then press between absorbent paper. Or soak ink stains immediately in milk.

. . . .

Dried ink stains—rub with a cut tomato and wash well.

. . . .

To remove beet stains from clothes, rub half a cut pear over the mark.

. . . .

Remove wash-in hair color on a towel by spraying with hairspray.

• • • •

Lipstick stains on clothing can be removed by rubbing with a piece of stale bread. On washable material, soak in vinegar and water.

• • • •

Orange juice or tomato stains—sponge with a mixture of ¼ ounce (6 grams) borax in 1 pint (600 milliliters) tepid water.

• • • •

Blackcurrant or blackberry stains—if still wet can be rubbed with lemon juice. If the stain has dried, then soak in glycerin and wash in hot water.

• • • •

Soot—never rub soot from fabric; cover the area with salt, then brush with a stiff brush.

• • • •

Tar stains—to remove from unwashable material, make a paste of powdered Fuller's earth and turpentine. Rub in well around the stain. Leave to dry and then brush off with a clean stiff brush.

• • • •

Remove tar or oil stains from white socks by rubbing with toothpaste.

• • • •

On washable material, rub the tarred area with lard, butter, or salad oil. Scrape off any loose tar after a few hours.

• • • •

"The man who removes a mountain begins by removing small stones."—Unknown

Fresh blood stains—on washable clothes, immediately soak in cold water. Rub with soap and cold water, rinse well. Add a few drops of ammonia or hydrogen peroxide to the water if the stain is resistant.

• • • •

Dried blood—soak the stains overnight in biological washing powder and cold water or in 1 gallon (3.8 liters) water with 8 ounces (200 grams) salt added.

• • • •

Stubborn bloodstains—mix liquid dish soap with milk and apply to the stain.

• • • •

On unwashable fabric such as blankets, use a paste of raw starch and lukewarm water. Spread on the stain and, when paste is discolored, brush off with a soft brush.

• • • •

Grass stains—on jeans or pants, treat by rubbing gently with lemon juice before washing. On other material, dampen the stain with cold water, apply cream of tartar, and leave for a few hours.

• • • •

Tea and coffee stains—to remove from white tea towels, soak in water with a dissolved denture cleaning tablet. Sugar sprinkled over a fresh tea stain will make it easier to wash out.

• • • •

Bicycle oil—to remove from pants, massage the stain with liquid dish soap.

. . . .

Bicycle grease, suntan lotion, and gravy stains—use scented soap to remove stains from clothes.

. . . .

Dirty shirt collars—rub shampoo into the collars, leave for ten minutes, then wash as usual. Or apply a paste of vinegar and baking soda and leave for 15 minutes.

. . . .

Cooking oil or grease—dab on some talcum powder over the marks before washing.

. . . .

Urine stains—sponge with a solution of baking soda and water to neutralize the acid and remove the smell.

. . . .

Perspiration stains—soak garments in water with a dash of white vinegar or a handful of baking soda. Which method will work on your clothes depends on your body chemistry. Or dissolve a couple of crushed aspirin tablets in the washing water.

LAUNDRY

Before hanging out clothes in cold weather, wet your hands with vinegar and rub in until dry. This will prevent your hands from chapping.

. . . .

Rubbing cornstarch on your hands will help prevent your skin from cracking in the cold, dry air.

. . . .

Reduce excess soap suds in the washing machine by adding a dash of vinegar or lemon juice or a drop of fabric conditioner with half a cup of water to the powder compartment—the suds will disappear.

. . . .

Before using new towels, soak them in cold water overnight and then wash as normal.

. . . .

To stop jeans from fading, before the first wash, make a solution of 7 ounces (220 grams) salt to a bucket of warm water and soak the jeans for 24 hours. Then wash as normal. Or soak for 30 minutes in 1 gallon (3.8 liters) water with 4 tablespoons (60 milliliters) added vinegar.

. . . .

Rather than using expensive scented dryer sheets, use a clean cloth moistened with fabric conditioner.

. . . .

Add starch to the rinsing water when washing nylon tights or stockings to help prevent runs and snags.

. . . .

Always stretch new stockings before wearing to make them last longer.

. . . .

Buy nylon stockings that are a generous fit and remove jewelry before putting them on.

. . . .

Wash new tights or stockings in warm water, squeeze dry in a towel, and place them in a plastic bag. Put into the freezer overnight. Next day let them thaw out and then hang out to dry. This will prolong their life.

. . . .

Prevent fine nylon tights or stockings from getting runs by spraying them very lightly with hair spray.

. . . .

Wash silk gently by hand in a warm, soapy water solution. Rinse thoroughly, adding 4 tablespoons (60 milliliters) white vinegar to 1 gallon (3.8 liters) water for the final rinse. Iron while still damp.

. . . .

Wash mohair or lambswool garments with a mild hair shampoo, then add a little hair conditioner to the final rinse.

. . . .

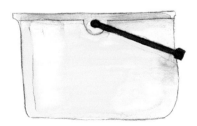

Place rubber bands around the cuffs of woolen garments after washing to avoid them being stretched.

. . . .

To wash gloves, put them on and scrub with a nail brush.

. . . .

Clean dishcloths by placing them in the silverware section of the dishwasher.

. . . .

Add 1 tablespoon (15 milliliters) sugar to hand-washing water and you will find that it helps to remove grime.

. . . .

Turn children's white socks inside out before washing to retain their whiteness.

. . . .

To remove annoying lint from clothes, gently comb with a razor and then brush with a clothes brush.

. . . .

To stop bright colored T-shirts or other clothes from fading, wash and dry them inside out.

. . . .

Stop color running into the white parts of multi-colored clothes by adding 1 tablespoon (15 milliliters) salt to the washing powder.

. . . .

To clean chamois leather, add a few drops of ammonia to a bowl of warm suds. Soak the chamois cloth in this for 15 minutes, squeeze gently, and transfer to another bowl of soapy water of the same temperature. Wash by squeezing gently. Rinse in warm water with 1 tablespoon (15 milliliters) olive oil added. Press between towels and pull into shape before hanging up to dry. When damp, rub with hands to make pliable.

. . . .

Place a clean towel over the washing line before hanging drip dry clothes on it. This prevents line marks from appearing on the garment.

. . . .

Use an old shoulder bag to carry clothespins when hanging out laundry to dry; this leaves both hands free.

IRONING

To reduce ironing, finish your wash on a short spin, then fold neatly and replace in machine on a fast spin.

. . . .

When drying clothes in the dryer, put a clean dry towel in with the wet clothes to make them less wrinkly.

. . . .

Iron collars from each corner towards the middle to prevent creasing.

. . . .

"Keeping your clothes well pressed will keep you from looking hard pressed." —Coleman Cox

Remove a permanent crease from material by sponging well with white vinegar and then press with a warm iron over a damp cloth.

• • • •

To remove stubborn creases when ironing, turn the garment inside out and place on a towel, then press.

• • • •

Add 1–2 drops of lavender or 1 teaspoon (5 milliliters) fabric conditioner to 1 pint (600 milliliters) of water and use to spray clothes before ironing.

• • • •

If a piece of plastic is stuck to an iron, unplug and allow to cool, then rub with nail polish remover.

• • • •

To clean a rusty iron, tie a piece of beeswax in a rag and rub the hot iron with the cloth. Then rub the surface with another cloth sprinkled with salt. This should remove any rust. Keep the waxed cloth for further use.

• • • •

To remove burnt and sticky residue from an iron, wrap a bar of soap in a handkerchief and rub over the base of the hot iron until smooth.

• • • •

Sprinkle a little salt on a piece of paper and run the hot iron over it to remove rough, sticky spots.

• • • •

To unblock a steam iron, pour a little vinegar into the empty water holder, switch on the iron, and let it heat up. By the time the liquid has evaporated the holes will be clear.

CURTAINS

Wash colored curtains or washable rugs in a saltwater solution to brighten the colors.

• • • •

Add a denture cleaning tablet to the water when washing sheer curtains to make them lovely and white.

• • • •

To wash lace curtains, fold them and rinse in clean water several times. Then put them into soapy water and squeeze well, but do not wring. When clean, rinse under a tap of cold running water. Rinse again in a bowl of hot water with starch added. Squeeze gently, unfold, and hang out to dry. When dry, fold the curtains across (not lengthways) and iron. Net curtains are washed the same way.

• • • •

To wash velveteen curtains, first shake well. Then put them into a bowl with plenty of warm soapy water and squeeze gently. Do not rub. Renew soapy water and repeat the process. Rinse in plenty of lukewarm water. Hang out without wringing and, when dry, brush the velvet with a soft brush or rub with a square of foam plastic.

• • • •

"Experience is something you get too late to do anything about the mistakes you made while getting it."—Unknown

Clean venetian or mini blinds by saturating a cloth with alcohol and wrapping it around a rubber spatula to clean both a bottom and a top slat at the same time.

• • • •

Clean venetian blinds by wearing an old fabric glove dipped in warm soapy water. Draw each slat between the fingers.

BEDDING

When washing blankets, choose a dry breezy day. Put 2 tablespoons (30 milliliters) borax and 1 pint (600 milliliters) of soft soap into a large tub of cold water. Make sure all is dissolved before putting in blankets. Leave the blankets in the water for about nine hours. Rub any stains and rinse well. Do not wring out (the blanket can be rinsed and spun on a short cycle in the washing machine). Hang out to dry.

• • • •

To make blankets mothproof, use 2 tablespoons (30 milliliters) of eucalyptus oil, ½ pint (300 milliliters) methylated spirits, and 8 ounces (225g) of soap flakes. Mix well and keep in a screw-top jar until needed. Add 1 tablespoon (15 milliliters) of the mixture to each 1 gallon (3.8 liters) water used and soak the blankets in this solution until clean. Spin or wring dry. Do not rinse. Dry outside on a breezy day if possible.

• • • •

A layer of newspapers under stored blankets will deter moths.

• • • •

When storing woolen blankets or winter woollies, place dried orange peel between the layers to give a nice smell and keep moths at bay.

• • • •

Duvets made of manmade materials —wash in a large washing machine but only use one-third of your usual amount of washing powder and wash at 104°F (40°C). Give four or five rinses. Spin in short bursts of 30 seconds. Dry outdoors if possible. Duvets can be tumble dried in warm air until the cover feels dry, then put in an airing cupboard for 24 hours before using.

• • • •

Feather pillows—launder in the washing machine. Place in dryer with a pair of tennis shoes. This pounds and fluffs the pillows but is noisy and can take longer than a single drying cycle. Feel the pillows with your fingers to make sure the feathers are dry and not matted. If you feel any lumps, return to drier.

• • • •

When packing electric blankets away, store them laid out flat between the mattress and the bed-base.

CLEANING HINTS

Melt a crushed aspirin in 1 cup (250 milliliters) of warm water and add 1 tablespoon (15 milliliters) methylated spirits to a bucket of water. Use this solution to clean doorsteps in frosty weather and they will not freeze and become slippery.

. . . .

An all-purpose cleaner for painted walls: wear rubber gloves and mix 1 cup (250 milliliters) ammonia, ½ cup (125 milliliters) vinegar, and ¼ cup (62.5 milliliters) baking soda with 1 gallon (3.8 liters) warm water. Wash thoroughly and rinse.

. . . .

Use WD40 (spray lubricant) to remove wax crayon from painted walls. Spray on and wipe off immediately. Rub scented soap on the wall to remove all traces of the lubricant. Heavily colored areas should be done a few times or sprayed and left for a while.

. . . .

Remove black condensation damp or mold by rubbing the area with an old toothbrush dipped in a mild solution of household bleach. Wipe with a damp cloth.

. . . .

Soften old chamois leather cloths by rinsing them in 4 pints (2.5 liters) of water with 1 teaspoon (5 milliliters) of olive oil added.

. . . .

"What most of us need most is to need less."—Unknown

Urine odors on a mattress may be neutralized by dampening the spot and sprinkling with borax. Rub the borax into the area and let dry. Brush or vacuum to remove the dry borax. Pet urine and sour milk odors can be neutralized using the same process.

• • • •

Remove pet hairs from fabric by putting on a pair of thick household rubber gloves and rubbing your hands over the surface of chairs, carpets, etc.

• • • •

Clean leather bags by rubbing them with the inside of a banana skin or with a cloth dipped in egg white whisked until frothy. Polish with a soft cloth.

• • • •

Revive shabby suede shoes by sponging with vinegar. Stuff with newspaper and leave to dry. Rub lightly with sandpaper and then with a stiff brush.

• • • •

Buff polished leather shoes with an old pair of tights.

FLOOR COVERINGS

Use water from boiled potatoes to freshen discolored carpets. This also helps to remove mud stains from carpets. Rinse with clean water.

• • • •

To restore and brighten carpet colors, sprinkle a mixture of tea leaves and salt over the whole carpet, then vacuum or brush off.

. . . .

Make your own carpet cleaner by adding 2 tablespoons (30 milliliters) each of salt and white vinegar to a bowl of warm soapy water.

. . . .

For a wine stain on a carpet, soak up the excess as quickly as possible. Cover the stain with an absorbent powder such as salt or talcum powder. When the powder becomes sticky, remove it and add more until most of the stain has gone. Apply a final layer of powder and leave for two hours, then brush this off. Any remaining marks can be removed by rubbing with a cloth dampened in a mild detergent solution. Rinse with a clean wet cloth, rub dry, and air well.

. . . .

Burn marks on carpets: slight marks caused by sparks can be removed by rubbing vigorously with the cut surface of a raw onion or a raw potato.

. . . .

Discarded nylon tights are good for cleaning nylon-based stair carpets. Dampen the tights in warm water and wipe the stair carpet.

. . . .

Remove stains from darker carpets by rubbing with used coffee grounds. Brush in well, allow to dry, then vacuum as usual.

. . . .

Dried coffee stains: remove from a carpet by rubbing a few drops of glycerin into the mark to loosen it, then leave for a few hours. Squeeze out a cloth in warm water with a little liquid dish soap added, and wipe the area.

• • • •

Table salt will absorb spilled ink. Pour salt on the wet ink and continue to add salt until there is no more wet ink. Then vacuum or wash.

• • • •

Milk stains: mix six parts water, two parts ammonia and a pinch of salt, dampen a soft cloth with this solution, and use to remove the stains.

• • • •

Fresh coffee stains: remove with saltwater.

• • • •

Lambskin rugs: brush with plenty of dry powdered magnesia. Leave for a day, shake well, and brush thoroughly.

. . . .

Clean the brushes on the vacuum cleaner with a dog's metal comb.

. . . .

Empty a vacuum cleaner bag onto a wet newspaper to avoid the dust blowing around.

. . . .

To make the vacuum cleaner cord rewind more easily, spray a little polish onto a cloth and pull along the lead.

. . . .

If the extension tube of your vacuum cleaner becomes slack and tends to fall out, give the joints a tighter fit by rubbing around the inner tube with a candle. Or wrap a strong elastic band around it to tighten the connection.

. . . .

Crayon marks on vinyl can be removed with silver polish. On wallpaper, rub very gently with washing soda sprinkled on a damp cloth. On hard surfaces, rub lightly with a dry soap-filled steel wool pad. Do not wet.

. . . .

Ballpoint pen ink can be removed from vinyl by rubbing with a slice of raw potato.

. . . .

To clean linoleum: wear household gloves and make a solution of ½ cup (125 milliliters) of household bleach and ¼ cup (62.5 milliliters) each of white vinegar and washing soda. Add this to 1 gallon (3.8 liters) warm water. Use the solution to mop your linoleum floor.

• • • •

To brighten old linoleum, mix one part of fresh milk with one part turpentine. Rub the mixture onto the floor and polish with a warmed soft cloth.

• • • •

To clean floor and wall tiles, dissolve 4 ounces (100 grams) of shredded coarse soap and 4 ounces (100 grams) washing soda in 1 gallon (3.8 liters) hot water. Scrub the tiles with the solution and a stiff brush. Rinse and dry.

WOOD

Black streaks on banister rails or tops of chairs can be removed by mixing equal drops of turpentine and vinegar with enough powdered laundry starch to make a paste. Carefully rub the area with the mixture. Rinse off with warm water.

• • • •

To clean a wood block floor, rub lightly with a fine steel wool pad moistened with turpentine substitute. Rub with the grain. As the polish and grime softens the dirt, wipe it off. Re-polish when dry.

• • • •

Black heel marks on light-colored floors can be removed with white spirit or turpentine.

. . . .

Pen marks on wood, plastic, or other hard surfaces can be removed by using cotton balls dipped in aftershave.

. . . .

Clean varnished woodwork or floors with cold tea. Then polish with a soft duster.

. . . .

To remove slight water marks on polished wood, rub with a cloth dipped in metal polish, then use wax polish to shine.

. . . .

To remove large water marks on polished wood, rub with an equal mixture of linseed oil and turpentine substitute.

. . . .

White ring marks on tables from wet or hot dishes or glasses can be removed by rubbing a thin paste of vegetable oil and salt on the spot with your fingers. Leave for a couple of hours then wipe it off.

. . . .

Use lavender furniture polish on woodwork for a fresh smell and to discourage flies.

. . . .

To avoid getting metal polish on stained wood when cleaning a mail slot on a door, wipe the wood around the brass with paper towel dipped in cooking oil. After polishing, wipe off the oil with clean paper towel.

• • • •

To remove paper stuck on wood, moisten with baby oil and leave for a few minutes; it will peel off easily.

• • • •

To clean cork table placemats, put them in a bowl of clean cold water and rub each one gently with a pumice stone. Rinse under cold running water. Dry in a cool place. Do not use soap or warm water.

CLEANING CONCOCTIONS

Be sure to store all cleaning solutions out of reach of young children and pets.

• • • •

Carpet cleaner: dissolve 2 ounces (50 grams) of yellow washing soap in 2 pints (1.2 liters) boiling water, then add ½ ounce (2.5 grams) washing soda and 3 tablespoons (45 milliliters) ammonia. Mix thoroughly and pour into carefully labeled jars. Mix 2 tablespoons (30 milliliters) of the mixture in 2 pints (1.2 liters) warm water and rub onto the carpet with a brush or cloth. Rinse off with a clean water and cloth. Dry well with a dry cloth. Open the windows and doors to air the carpet. Do not saturate the carpet or the backing will rot.

• • • •

"To scrub a floor has alleviated many a broken heart." —*Unknown*

Non-slip sheen for wooden floors: mix equal parts of paraffin oil and vinegar in a screw-top plastic jar, shake well, and apply sparingly to the floor with a dry cloth. Repeat monthly.

• • • •

Furniture polish: mix two parts of boiled linseed oil with one part each of white vinegar, turpentine, and methylated spirit. Whisk well together. Store in a firmly corked and clearly labeled bottle. Shake well before use.

• • • •

Make a polishing cloth: mix 3 tablespoons (45 milliliters) each of paraffin (or linseed) oil and vinegar in a screw-top jar. Put a duster into the jar to absorb the liquid. Then hang out to dry. Use to polish furniture and store in the jar when not in use.

• • • •

Silver dip: half fill a 32-ounce jar with silver paper (chocolate bar wrappers are best). Add 2 tablespoons (30 milliliters) cooking salt and fill the jar with cold water. Cover the jar and keep near the kitchen sink. Dip stained silver silverware in the mixture and leave for two minutes to remove any stains. Rinse thoroughly.

• • • •

Brass polish: mix ½ teaspoon (2.5 milliliters) salt and ½ cup (125 milliliters) white vinegar with enough plain flour to make a paste. Apply the polish to the brass and leave for half an hour. Rub and wipe off with clean cloth.

• • • •

Chrome polish: use apple cider vinegar. Wet a cloth with the vinegar, wipe on the chrome. Dry with a clean towel.

. . . .

Copper polish: Mix together lemon juice and salt. Apply to the copper and scrub with scouring pad.

METALS

Silver: use pieces of raw rhubarb for cleaning silver. Or place silver in potato cooking water until it shines.

. . . .

Tarnished silver articles: add 1 teaspoon (5 milliliters) baking soda and 1 teaspoon (5 milliliters) salt to 1 pint (600 milliliters) of almost boiling water. Immerse silver in it and leave until tarnish has disappeared. Rinse in warm water and dry with a soft cloth. Or crumple some tin foil and place it in a bowl of water. Put the silver in the water and let it soak for a couple of hours.

. . . .

Tarnished silver with intricate patterns: clean using toothpaste on a soft toothbrush.

. . . .

Dull gold jewelry: to bring instant shine, rub with a cut tomato. Rinse well.

• • • •

Stained silver jewelry: silver jewelry damaged by bleach or perming solution stains will gleam if soaked in vinegar for a few hours then rubbed with a dry cloth.

• • • •

Pewter: clean by rubbing with the pithy side of a piece of orange or cabbage leaves. Polish with a soft cloth.

• • • •

Rusty or tarnished brass curtain hooks: soak them in ammonia, then boil in the water in which haricot beans have been cooked.

• • • •

Neglected brass will clean easier if it is first washed in a solution of strong ammonia. Or leave the article in a cola drink overnight.

• • • •

Brass ornaments: clean using a dash of cider on a cloth.

• • • •

Dirty brass and copper: bring back the shine by rubbing with half a lemon dipped in salt. Wash well in soapy water and rinse thoroughly before giving a good buff.

• • • •

When using store-bought brass cleaner, add some lemon juice for better results.

. . . .

A soft cloth dipped in white spirit makes an economical cleaner for brass.

. . . .

Polish brass with a soft cloth and a few drops of olive oil. Rinse off with water and liquid dish soap. Finally, polish with a clean cloth.

. . . .

After polishing brass, give it a quick rub with flour for a longer lasting shine. Or spray with hair spray. Protect any surrounding wooden area with newspaper first.

. . . .

Lacquered or varnished brass should never be scoured. Instead, apply a paste of lemon juice and cream of tartar. Leave for five minutes and then wash with warm water and dry thoroughly with a soft cloth.

. . . .

Tobacco stains: clean stains from brass or nickel ashtrays by applying alcohol with an old toothbrush and then washing in hot vinegar and salt.

. . . .

Bronze: to clean bronze, dust well and rub the surface with a little warmed linseed oil. Polish with a chamois leather. Avoid using water or white spirits on bronze.

. . . .

Chrome: Rub with a damp cloth and dry starch or baking soda. Rinse, dry thoroughly, and polish well.

. . . .

Chromium plated taps, etc.: rub occasionally with a cloth dipped in paraffin to keep them gleaming.

. . . .

Rust on stainless steel shelves: rub with lighter fluid, then clean with regular kitchen cleaner. Or remove spots on stainless steel with white vinegar.

. . . .

Rusted iron or steel: soak in paraffin for one to two days to soften the rust. Gently rub the wet surface with emery paper.

GLASS

Clean electric light bulbs regularly with a cloth moistened with methylated spirits.

. . . .

To remove fly spots from electric bulbs, dampen soft paper towel in a mixture of equal amounts of vinegar and water, then rub this over the bulbs.

. . . .

Rub the inside of fish tanks with salt to remove hard water deposits, then rinse well before returning the fish to the tank. Use only plain, not iodized, salt.

. . . .

Never clean the glass in a picture frame with a damp cloth as the water can seep into the picture and cause damage. Instead, use paper towel dampened with methylated spirit. Use this method for mirrors, too.

• • • •

Window cleaning solution: 1 teaspoon (5 milliliters) of household ammonia and 1 tablespoon (15 milliliters) methylated spirits in 1 pint (600 milliliters) water. Store in a clearly labeled plastic spray bottle for easy application.

• • • •

Another window cleaning solution: mix 3 tablespoons (45 milliliters) white vinegar (or methylated spirits) with 4 pints (2.5 liters) water. Apply with a clean cloth. Dry off with a chamois leather or a crumpled sheet of newspaper.

• • • •

Crumple old newspaper into a ball and slightly dampen it, then use to clean windows. Polish off with crumpled dry newspaper.

• • • •

To reduce condensation on windows in cold weather, place a cup of salt on the windowsill to absorb the room's moisture. Or rub a little glycerin over the inside of windows once a week.

• • • •

Rub lavender essential oil over windows and frames to keep flies out of the kitchen.

• • • •

Wash windows at a shady time of day. Wear sunglasses when cleaning windows and you'll see the smears more easily.

• • • •

After washing outside windowsills, spray them with furniture polish and they will stay cleaner for longer.

• • • •

When stacking delicate glass bowls on top of each other, put a folded piece of paper towel in the bottom of each dish. This avoids breakage and keeps the bowls from sticking together.

• • • •

To make inexpensive glassware sparkle, rub a paste of baking soda and water on the glass. Rinse under cold running water. Dry and polish with a soft cloth.

• • • •

Rub down a small chip on the rim of a precious wine glass with emery paper to smooth it.

• • • •

Keep cut glass and crystal vases clean by lining with a clear plastic bag before each use.

• • • •

To clean a badly stained, narrow-necked vase, tear up newspaper and place in the vase. Fill with warm water. Leave overnight and shake the paper around, then empty the vase and rinse well. Or put a strong salt solution in the vase and shake, then wash the vase with soap and water. Or clean with a solution of a name brand of toilet cleaner diluted in a little water. Leave for an hour and rinse well before use.

• • • •

If a stopper is jammed in the neck of a decanter, put a few drops of cooking oil or glycerin around the rim and leave overnight. Tapping the stopper gently with the back of a wooden brush will often remove it.

• • • •

To clean a decanter or carafe, fill with warm water and 1 tablespoon (15 milliliters) baking soda. Add some crushed eggshells or rice grains. Leave for several hours, shaking regularly. Rinse with hot water and dry in the sun. Or use a solution of equal amounts of warm water and vinegar with half a cup of sand. Shake well and leave overnight. Rinse well.

• • • •

Lime stains caused by hard water can be removed in the same way as above but use tea leaves with the vinegar.

. . . .

To remove wine stains from a decanter, add chopped raw potato and warm water, shake vigorously for a few minutes. Or add a little ammonia to the washing water and scrub with a brush. Rinse well.

GENERAL CLEANING

Tapestry: sprinkle with powdered magnesia and work it in well with a clean cloth held between your fingertips. Leave overnight or for several hours, then brush out gently with a soft clean brush.

. . . .

Remove marks from old china and porcelain by painting with neat bleach, or rub brown marks with a damp cloth dipped in salt until they disappear.

. . . .

To clean the inside of a clock, soak a small piece of a cotton ball in kerosene or paraffin and place in the base of the clock. Leave for a few days. This will draw down all the dust and leave the clock clean.

. . . .

"It's better to lose sleep on what you plan to do than to be kept awake by what you have done."—Unknown

Ivory piano keys: clean with a little toothpaste on a damp cloth. Use milk to rinse. Polish off with a soft cloth. Or rub with a cloth sprinkled with hydrogen peroxide or pure lemon juice. Never use water on ivory. If possible, leave keys exposed to sunlight as they yellow in the dark. Sprinkle French chalk between the keys to prevent them from sticking.

• • • •

Gilt picture frames: mix one egg white with 1 teaspoon (5 milliliters) baking soda. Sponge the surface with the mixture. Or use a little dry cleaning fluid on a cloth.

• • • •

Wax crayon can be removed from most surfaces with white spirit, methylated spirit, or liquid sliver polish.

• • • •

Plaster statuettes: to remove dirt and grease, mix a paste of finely powdered starch and hot water. Apply the hot paste with a brush. Leave to dry; the starch will absorb the grime and flake off.

• • • •

Keep plastic or metal curtain tracks running smoothly by spraying them with silicone spray polish. If metal rails are slightly rusty, rub them with talcum powder or French chalk.

• • • •

Leather furniture: to prevent it from drying out, mix two parts raw linseed oil with one part wine vinegar. Shake well and apply evenly with a soft cloth, then polish.

. . . .

Use a broad clean paintbrush to dust the tops and fronts of books stacked on a shelf.

. . . .

Spray polish onto the inside of your dustpan to ensure collected dust is easily removed.

. . . .

Marble: clean by painting the surface with a mixture of one part powdered pumice, one part powdered chalk, and two parts baking soda. Leave on for a day and wash off with clean water and a soft brush. Or wash with a strong solution of saltwater with an added dash of vinegar.

. . . .

To remove green algae from a headstone, wash with a solution of one part hydrogen peroxide to three parts water, plus a few drops of ammonia. Rinse well with water.

. . . .

Oil stains from a concrete driveway: remove by pouring a little cola drink over them to dissolve the mark.

. . . .

Grease or oil on concrete: clean by putting kitty litter over the stain. Leave to soak up the grease, then sweep up. Alternatively, shake dry laundry detergent on the grease, dampen the powder, and leave to absorb the grease. Wash off with water.

. . . .

Concrete stained with black coloration from the weather is usually mold. Spray a solution of one part bleach to three parts water on the concrete. Brush in and leave for a few hours. Wash off with clean water.

Home Decorating and Gardening

WALLPAPERING

When stripping wallpaper, use a small amount of wallpaper paste mixed with warm water and a squirt of liquid dish soap. Soak the paper in this for a while; the liquid dish soap acts as a wetting agent, and the paste holds it in place.

. . . .

When measuring lengths of wallpaper, use Blu Tack to hold the top of the paper to the wall while you mark the correct length.

. . . .

If you need to apply a patch of wallpaper, tear the paper rather than cutting it. The join will be much less noticeable that way.

. . . .

When decorating, use a plastic mop bucket to hold the wallpaper paste. Rest the brush in the wringer part and any drips will fall into the bucket.

. . . .

Blu Tack will come away from wallpaper without tearing if you warm it with a hairdryer for a few seconds first.

. . . .

Decorate cardboard boxes with leftover wallpaper and use them for storage on top of the wardrobe.

. . . .

For paper hanging: use a paint roller for smoothing down the paper instead of a brush.

. . . .

"Lots of people know a good thing the moment somebody else sees it first."
—Unknown

After wallpapering, rinse the paste brushes in salted water before washing them. This removes the paste more easily and leaves the brushes soft and springy.

• • • •

When you're done wallpapering, pour a little leftover paste into a jar with a plastic lid and use to paste any missed corners and edges that haven't stuck properly.

• • • •

To stick down curling corners of wallpaper, paint the back with egg white. Leave until tacky and then press down firmly.

PAINTING

Before painting, run a comb through the paintbrush to remove any loose bristles.

• • • •

To soften a paintbrush hardened with paint, suspend the bristles in raw linseed oil for a day. Rinse in warm turpentine substitute and work the bristles with fingers (wear gloves) to remove softened deposits. Rinse well.

• • • •

If the bristles of a paintbrush are bent, hold them over a steaming kettle for a few minutes, then pull them back into shape.

• • • •

"The only real mistake is the one from which we learn nothing."—Unknown

When soaking paintbrushes, clip a clothes peg onto the handle to prevent the bristles from resting on the bottom of the jar.

· · · ·

Boil a few onions in 3 pints (1.8 liters) of water until very soft. Drain and reserve the water and use with or without soap to clean white paint.

· · · ·

Cut an old loofah into pieces and use with detergent to clean paint work without scratching.

· · · ·

When painting doors, remember to paint along the top, as this is where dust accumulates. It will be easier to wipe if covered with gloss paint.

· · · ·

When painting or varnishing an outside door, take the door off and paint the bottom—rainwater that runs down the door and seeps underneath can cause rotting.

· · · ·

After painting a door and allowing it to dry, rub the door edges with a candle to prevent the door from sticking. Or put a film of talcum powder around the door edge.

· · · ·

When painting windows, protect the glass from paint by placing strips of dampened newspaper along the inside edges. It is easily removed when the job is done.

. . . .

To stop newly painted windows from sticking to the frame, allow the paint to dry and spray both painted edges with furniture polish. Rub gently with a cloth before closing the window.

. . . .

Make it easier to paint awkward corners of window frames by fixing an elastic band tightly around the top of the bristles of the brush to bind them closer together.

. . . .

When spray painting something awkward like a bicycle, cover the parts you don't want sprayed with plastic wrap.

. . . .

Stand enamel or lacquer paint in hot water for 30 minutes before use to make it easier to apply.

. . . .

If paint has gone lumpy, strain through muslin or old nylon stockings.

. . . .

Cover the paint tray with aluminum foil or a plastic bag when painting with a roller. This can be disposed of afterwards, leaving a paint-free tray.

. . . .

Messy painters should stand the paint can on a paper plate to catch the drips.

. . . .

When filling in cracks in walls before painting, mix the filler with the water based paint to be used. Then it should only take one coat to cover the repaired area. Always add plaster or filler to the liquid.

. . . .

When painting cellar steps, add a little sand to the paint to give a better grip on the treads.

. . . .

When painting is finished, pour any leftover paint into a screw-top glass jar. No skin will form and it can be used to repair scratches.

. . . .

When finished with a paint can, smear a little petroleum jelly around the rim before replacing the lid. This will make it easier to reopen.

. . . .

Rub margarine, lard, or olive oil plus a spoonful of granulated sugar into hands to remove gloss paints. Wipe with newspaper, then wash as usual.

• • • •

Nail polish remover will take wood varnish off your hands without leaving your skin dry or smelly.

D.I.Y. HINTS

Nail an old thread spool to the floor to act as a doorstop. Paint it to match the floor covering.

• • • •

Use cotton swabs when grouting tiles. The soft head gathers up excess cement and leaves smooth lines. They can also get into awkward corners.

• • • •

If a wall tile falls off and you have run out of glue, heat some jam to boiling point. Then, using a paintbrush, apply the jam to the back of the tile. Hold in place for a few minutes and it will stick fast.

• • • •

When putting up ceiling tiles, use a soft paint roller to put firm, even pressure on them to stick. This also stops finger marks in the tiles.

. . . .

Repair small holes in vinyl or linoleum floor covering with a wax crayon. Find a crayon of matching color and melt it with a match or lighter, being careful not to blacken the wax. Allow the wax to drip into the hole. When the crayon sets hard, scrape off any protruding wax to make it level with the floor.

. . . .

Use fabric dye to stain wood to any color you like. Mix the dye using half the recommended amount of water stated on the packet. Allow to cool before brushing onto the wood. This is particularly effective on white wood.

. . . .

Use an old icing bag with a small, plain nozzle to fill the cracks between floor boards.

. . . .

Level out freshly applied bath sealant with an ice cube for a smooth finish.

. . . .

When hanging a picture on a wall, wrap some adhesive tape around the center of the cord to keep it from slipping.

. . . .

Stop floorboards squeaking by shaking French chalk or talcum powder between them.

. . . .

When laying rubber-backed carpet on a tiled floor, cover the tiles with newspaper or brown paper first to prevent it from sticking to the floor.

. . . .

If you need frosted windows for more privacy, make up a solution of 1 tablespoon (15 milliliters) Epsom salts to 1 cup beer. Brush on the window and leave to dry. To remove the frost, wash off with ammonia. Cover any wood or nearby furniture first to avoid them getting splashed.

. . . .

Soften hardened putty by putting it in a plastic bag and placing it in hot water for a short time.

. . . .

Stop birds from eating freshly set window putty by adding some black pepper to it when mixing.

. . . .

Store unused putty wrapped up in foil then placed in a tub so that it lasts longer.

. . . .

Remove putty from around a window by applying paraffin oil to it. This dissolves the linseed oil in the putty and it will soon crumble away.

. . . .

If you have no oil, stop a creaking door by applying a few drops of liquid dish soap or non-stick vegetable oil spray to the hinges. Or use Vaseline.

· · · ·

When keys won't turn in a rusty lock, pour cola into it.

· · · ·

Remove self-adhesive hooks from doors by warming with a hairdryer to loosen the glue. Pry off the hook with a blunt knife and remove any remaining glue with white spirit.

· · · ·

Use an electric carving knife to cut foam rubber to shape for DIY seating.

· · · ·

If you need to apply oil to hard-to-reach places, fit a plastic straw over the nozzle of the oil can.

· · · ·

To remember where wires go when wiring a plug: bLue to the left (L for left), bRown to the right (R for right).

· · · ·

Before sawing through a piece of wood, apply a little liquid dish soap to the blade of the saw.

· · · ·

To stop plywood splitting when sawing it, lay masking tape over the area to be cut.

. . . .

When using a ladder, always make sure that the foot of the ladder is one measure out for every four measures in height.

. . . .

Ladders must be placed on a firm level surface, and the top should be resting on something solid, and not on gutters or a windowsill.

. . . .

When painting and decorating, put old socks over the ends of the ladder to avoid marking the walls.

. . . .

When drilling, mark with a crayon or place a small rubber band or masking tape around the bit to the depth you want the hole. Drill until the band reaches the surface of the wood and you will have the correct depth.

. . . .

When drilling masonry, always withdraw the tip every five seconds to keep it from overheating. If you don't keep the tip cool it can damage the drill. Or squirt water into the hole. The water helps the drilling process.

. . . .

When drilling sheet glass or mirrors, mark your spot with a felt tip pen. Make a small well out of putty over the marked spot and fill this with a touch of light oil. Drill slowly using a carbide tipped drill bit. The oil keeps the drill bit cool and makes the job easier.

. . . .

To stop a tile from cracking when inserting a Rawlplug through a drilled hole in a glazed tile, make sure that the plug has passed through the tile before you insert the screw.

. . . .

Before putting nails or screws into wood, lubricate them on a bar of soap. They will insert more easily.

. . . .

A saw will cut wood more smoothly if the teeth are rubbed with soap.

. . . .

Short lengths of hollow plastic clothesline or matches can be used instead of wall plugs.

. . . .

Cover a screw with oil before inserting it. It's easier to take out later, plus this prevents rusting.

. . . .

Brass and chrome screws are not very strong, so first make a hole with a smaller sized nail or a wood screw of the same size.

. . . .

To loosen rusted screws, soak overnight in lemon juice. A tissue wrapped round the area keeps the juice where it can do its work.

. . . .

If you are trying to remove a very rusty screw, use the tip of a very hot soldering iron to heat the head of the screw. The heat should expand the screw head and loosen the rust.

. . . .

If you damage a tight screw when trying to remove it, use a junior hacksaw blade to cut a new groove.

. . . .

Renew rusty screws and nails by soaking them overnight in a container of neat vinegar. Rinse and dry thoroughly in an oven set on a low heat.

. . . .

To loosen a screw or nut that has been painted over, dab on nail polish remover and leave for a few minutes.

. . . .

To help tighten a loose screw, wrap some wire wool around the threads and then reinsert it.

. . . .

If you haven't got a crosshead screwdriver to remove screws, use the tip of a potato peeler.

. . . .

When opening a piece of equipment, keep the removed screws in the correct sequence by poking them into a piece of Blu Tack or beeswax.

. . . .

When trying to free bolts that have gone rusty, pour some cola drink over them and leave for a few hours.

. . . .

Knock in small tacks and panel pins easily by using an old comb to hold them in place.

. . . .

Try not to run a line of nails along the same wood grain, otherwise the wood could split. If you have to, then drill several guide holes in advance.

. . . .

Glass jars with screw-on metal lids make excellent storage jars. Drill two holes in the lids and attach to the underside of the shelves in your garage. Sort, label, and store nails and other small parts in the jars and screw on to the lids.

. . . .

When hammering tacks into furniture, protect the upholstery by crisscrossing a few strips of first aid adhesive tape over the head of the hammer.

. . . .

The bags of silica gel usually given with electronic purchases should be kept and put in your tool box to keep the contents shiny.

. . . .

Attach an empty plastic box to the top rung of the stepladder as a handy toolbox.

. . . .

After redecorating the house, keep a list of the rolls of wallpaper used for each room, the length of the carpet required, the color, brand, and amount of paint used. This is not only very handy when next decorating, but also useful for new occupants if you should move.

GARDEN PESTS

Companion plants can deter pests.
- To reduce greenfly: grow garlic near roses, nasturtiums beside brassica, and chives with lettuce.
- To discourage carrot fly: plant onions near carrots.
- Stop cabbage white butterflies from laying eggs: plant thyme, dill, chamomile, and rosemary in the garden.
- Deter whitefly by planting French marigolds alongside fuchsias and tomatoes.
- Hoverflies are attracted to the flowers of marigolds, dill, and fennel, and since their larvae feed on greenfly, it is useful to encourage them into the garden.

. . . .

Make an environmentally friendly insecticide by boiling a handful of stinging nettles in 1 pint (600 milliliters) water. (Wear gloves when picking and handling nettles.) Leave the nettles to infuse for four days, then strain the liquid into a spray bottle.

. . . .

Save potted plants from hungry garden slugs by smearing petroleum jelly around the rims of the pots.

· · · ·

Sprinkle plain bran around plants to keep snails and slugs away.

· · · ·

To stop cats from soiling the flower beds, save used teabags and dry them, then add a few drops of Olbas oil to each one and place around the base of shrubs or plants. Alternatively, scatter orange peel around, as cats dislike the smell.

· · · ·

Stop cats from disturbing indoor plants by smearing lemongrass oil around the rims of the pots.

· · · ·

Douse aphids with potato water to which some liquid dish soap has been added.

· · · ·

Soot spread on the garden deters slugs, while snails can be trapped using saucers of beer.

· · · ·

Insect spray: dissolve 1 ounce (25 grams) of household soap in 1 pint (600 milliliters) water and bring to a boil. Add immediately to 2 pints (1.2 liters) of paraffin oil and whisk until it forms into an emulsion. For ordinary insects, dilute water 1:15. For "scale" insects, dilute 1:9. For soft insects such as plant lice, dilute 1:20.

GARDENING TIPS

Before starting to garden, pull your nails along a bar of soap until there's a layer underneath. This allows the nails to be easily cleaned when work has finished.

• • • •

Sprinkle gravel over the soil in window boxes and hanging baskets. This will prevent windows being splashed with mud during heavy showers.

• • • •

Use leftover carpet underlay to line hanging baskets; it will absorb the water.

• • • •

Save on compost for hanging baskets by lining them with used teabags. They make an excellent lining and fertilizer and retain the water well.

• • • •

Put old sponges in the bottom of flower baskets or pots; this way there is less watering as they retain their moisture.

• • • •

In large pots, save on compost by first placing a layer of broken pottery, then broken up plastic seedling trays, to one third of the depth of the pot.

• • • •

To save on compost and leave plant tubs lighter to move, fill the container with empty plastic bottles to a depth of 8 inches (20 centimeters). Cover with a layer of plastic, making holes for drainage. Fill to the top with compost.

· · · ·

When planting in terracotta garden pots, line with bubble plastic before adding the soil. This will stop them from cracking in the cold weather and also protects the roots of any perennial you may keep in them.

· · · ·

Generally shrubs and small trees like large containers as this allows more root room, which produces sturdier plants, holds moisture longer, and keeps the soil temperature more even.

· · · ·

To avoid the spread of plant diseases and pests when reusing a container, always give it a good clean with a mild disinfectant solution, then rinse well.

· · · ·

Avoid using ordinary garden soil in plant pots as it will compact and cause drainage problems. Soil-free composts tend to dry out quickly and are difficult to re-moisten. A good loam-based soil suits most plants.

· · · ·

To bring out the deep colors in roses, scatter crushed eggshells around their roots.

· · · ·

"The grass may be greener next door but it is just as hard to cut."
—Unknown

After boiling fish, save the water. When it's cool, pour it around your rose bushes for lovely blooms.

. . . .

If you have an aquarium, save the water each time you change it and water your houseplants with it.

. . . .

Put banana skins under the soil before planting roses. They rot quickly and provide nourishment.

. . . .

Cut the center from toilet paper or paper towel rolls into 1 inch (5 centimeter) segments, stand on a tray, and fill with soil. These are ideal for starting runner beans or sweet peas and make transplanting easy. The cardboard soon dissolves.

. . . .

Newspapers placed at the bottom of a seed tray help to retain moisture.

. . . .

Watering seedlings from a watering can may flatten them. Use a spray gun instead.

. . . .

When sowing, use a dampened matchstick or cocktail stick to pick out individual seeds for even distribution.

. . . .

Collect autumn leaves in sacks, put a brick on each one, and by spring your free leaf-mold is ready for use.

. . . .

Lift and divide most perennials every fourth year, in the autumn.

. . . .

Soak old newspapers and bury them in the garden; they will quickly rot and act as compost to enrich the soil.

. . . .

Sprinkle some Epsom salt crystals around the base of irises in the summer for better flowers the following year.

. . . .

After buying roses, soak them in a bucket of water overnight to give them a good drink before planting.

. . . .

Tie up delicate plants with strips of rolled up plastic wrap instead of special plant ties.

. . . .

To improve the appearance of a thin, straggly hedge, grow a flowering climber through it to add color, scent, and thickness.

. . . .

When trimming hedges, place a large cardboard box just below where you are cutting. This will catch most of the clippings.

. . . .

Pour salt into path or patio cracks to keep them free of weeds and grass. Or save the water from cooking potatoes and pour it over the cracks.

. . . .

Brush down patio and garden paths with a solution of biological washing powder.

. . . .

Remove green fungi from a cement path or patio by pouring on water containing bleach, then scrubbing with a brush.

When choosing bedding plants, remember:
- An annual will last for only one growing season.
- A biennial will last for only two years.
- A perennial plant will survive for longer than two years.

. . . .

Soak seeds in a cup of cool tea, then place into the refrigerator for three days before planting.

. . . .

Plant flower or vegetable seeds individually in used teabags. Keep them moist in a warm place until germinated. Transfer to pots or the garden by planting the entire teabag. This way the roots are not disturbed.

. . . .

After sowing seeds, pop the empty packet into a glass jar and place it upside down at the end of the row.

. . . .

Leeks grow better when a few handfuls of soot are added to the soil.

. . . .

Avoid watering cucumbers with cold or chlorinated water. Keep a container for water in your greenhouse or a warm room.

. . . .

Keep cucumbers dry at the point where they emerge from the ground to avoid "collar rot".

. . . .

Plant mint in a large pot, then sink it into the ground in the garden to stop the mint spreading.

. . . .

Treat mildew on plants with a solution of 2 teaspoons (10 grams) of baking soda to 1¾ pints (1 liter) water with a little liquid dish soap added to make it stick to the leaves.

. . . .

Mow your lawn regularly, never removing more than one third of the grass height per mowing. Keep your mower blade sharp. Dull blades will rip the grass, leaving the leaves with whitish tips.

. . . .

An old plastic tile-adhesive spreader makes a perfect scraper for the underside of lawn mowers and trimmers. Use the flat edge for general cleaning and the serrated edge for stubborn accumulations of grass cuttings. Always make sure that lawn mowers or trimmers are disabled before cleaning.

. . . .

Save compost from old grow-bags and line seed drills with it the following season.

. . . .

Gardeners will find it very useful if they mark off a long handled garden tool in centimeters and meters.

. . . .

A garden hose reels up more easily and won't crack if some hot water is run through it each time it's used

. . . .

Wear spiked golf shoes when mowing the grass as this aerates the lawn while you cut it.

. . . .

When planting a new tree, give it a dose of vitamin B to help it overcome the shock.

. . . .

If you have difficulty in growing a rock plant in a dry stone wall where there is little soil, wedge some wet cotton balls in the crevice, before placing the plant there. Use a long spouted watering can to keep the cotton balls moist until the plant starts to grow.

. . . .

When using creosote to treat wood fencing, extend the quantity by stirring in 1 pint (600 milliliters) paraffin to 1 gallon (3.8 liters) creosote.

FLOWERS

After purchasing or gathering flowers, put them in a bowl of lukewarm water and stand them in a dark place for an hour. Then arrange them in vases containing lukewarm water with a small pinch of baking soda added.

. . . .

Fresh flowers will keep better in a warm room if you add a couple of ice cubes to the water about twice a day.

. . . .

Keep flowers fresh by dipping the stems in boiling water for a few seconds.

. . . .

If you have few flowers but a big vase, stand a drinking glass in the vase, then arrange the flowers.

. . . .

"A cheerful thought, like a lovely flowe, can bring beauty to a day."
—Unknown

Put a handful of marbles or a round nylon pan scourer in the bottom of a vase to make flower arranging easier.

• • • •

When arranging spring flowers in a vase, keep daffodils and irises separate to prolong the life of each.

• • • •

Extend the life of carnations by keeping them in a cool place and adding a dash of soda water and a pinch of sugar to the water.

• • • •

Add a pinch of starch to the water in a vase before arranging tulips in it. This prevents them from drooping.

• • • •

To revive droopy tulips, use a pin to make a hole through the stem just below the flower. This will help them perk up. Alternatively, place a copper coin in the bottom of the vase.

• • • •

Roses should be cut early in the day before the dew has dried.

• • • •

The ends of woody stemmed flowers such as chrysanthemums or roses should be crushed with a heavy object or split before arranging—this makes them last longer.

• • • •

To revive wilting roses, wrap them in wet newspaper and place in a bucket of water overnight. Remove the paper in the morning and put them into a fresh vase of water.

• • • •

To preserve roses, gather the roses during the summer, just before they are in full bloom. Close the end of the stems with sealing wax, wrap the roses in tissue paper, and seal in an airtight box. The night before they are to be displayed, open the box, cut off the sealed ends, and leave the flowers in water overnight. They will look lovely and fresh next day.

• • • •

If cut roses don't open, put them in the microwave on a low setting for a few minutes, checking to prevent overdrying, and you will have lovely dried flowers.

• • • •

Half an aspirin tablet dissolved in a vase of drooping flowers will help revive them.

• • • •

Remove the lower leaves and split the ends of chrysanthemum stems before putting them in a vase. Put in a cool place at night to extend their life.

• • • •

When changing the water in a vase of fresh flowers, cut off ¼ inch (5 millimeters) from the stems before replacing them in the fresh water. The flowers will last much longer.

• • • •

Cut flower preservative: add 1 teaspoon (5 milliliters) baby bottle sterilizing liquid, 1 teaspoon alum, and 8 teaspoons (40 milliliters) sugar to 1 gallon (3.8 liters) of water. Reduce in proportion for smaller amounts. Do not change the water in the vase—just top it up.

• • • •

Mend a leaking vase with a few drops of melted candle wax.

• • • •

When beech leaves are at their brightest in the autumn, cut some branches and stand them in a mixture of half glycerin and half water to a depth of 1 inch (5 centimeters). When the liquid has been absorbed, they can be arranged in a dry vase as a decoration during the winter months.

• • • •

Extend the life of a dried flower arrangement by spraying lightly with hairspray.

INDOOR PLANTS

When potting houseplants, put a few bits of broken pottery in the base, then pack in used teabags, followed by the compost.

• • • •

When going on vacation, place an old towel or blanket in the bottom of the bath and soak thoroughly. Stand all your plants on it and they'll absorb moisture gradually and stay cool.

• • • •

"Judge each day, not by the harvest but by the seeds you plant."
—Unknown

To keep potted plants watered while away, drill a couple of tiny holes in the base of an empty plastic bottle. Push the bottle into the soil and fill with water. The water will slowly seep out and keep the soil moist.

• • • •

Cold tea makes an inexpensive and effective food for houseplants.

• • • •

To know when houseplants need watering, place a piece of tissue on top of the soil. When the paper is damp, the plant is okay, but when it is dry the plant requires water. Or dip a pencil into the soil—if it comes out dry with no dirt clinging, the plant needs water.

• • • •

Knitting needles (or the spokes from an old umbrella) make neat but strong supports for houseplants.

• • • •

Houseplants with large dust-attracting leaves should be sprayed with a water that has a few drops of baby oil added for a lasting shine.

• • • •

Use a sponge dipped in milk to clean the leaves of a rubber plant.

• • • •

If potted plants are looking a bit dusty, put them into the bath, then spray lightly with tepid water.

• • • •

Give your houseplants a good shine by polishing the leaves with the inside of a banana skin, then rub with a soft cloth.

• • • •

Save some seeds from small red peppers and plant two or three seeds at a time in small pots or cardboard egg boxes. When they are about 1 inch (5 centimeters) high, re-pot in a medium-sized plant pot. You will soon have an attractive indoor plant, and possibly a supply of chilies.

GARDEN TRIVIA

Years ago many gardeners kept bees and they hung juniper in the hives. They were advised to rub the inside and hive stands with hyssop, thyme, and fennel flowers so that the bees were happy in the hives and would always be glad to return to them.

• • • •

Many gardeners keep a toad in the garden or greenhouse to eat harmful insects.

• • • •

Mint and parsley, grown on windowsills, help to keep out flies and insects from the house.

• • • •

"We owe much to the garden spade. It gives a man one place where he can put his foot down."—Unknown

For many years, gardeners kept leeches to forecast the weather. They were kept in jars partly filled with water. If the leech lay still at the bottom of the jar, the weather would be good, if it crept to the top, rain was on the way. If the leech moved quickly, it would be windy, and if it stayed out of the water completely, heavy storms were imminent.

· · · ·

To avoid being plagued with tiny flies when out in the garden, take a yeast-free vitamin B complex. They don't seem to like it.

· · · ·

Rabbits can be a nuisance in the garden so here are some ways to deter them:

- Pour vinegar into a wide-necked jar and soak corn cobs (cut in half) in it for five minutes, then scatter the cobs across the vegetable or flower garden. Reuse the vinegar every two weeks to soak the cobs.
- Make a solution of cow manure and water and spray on the garden.
- Use red pepper, black pepper, cayenne, paprika, etc., as a dust to repel rabbits, as they are always sniffing.
- Mix 1 well-beaten egg, ½ teaspoon (2.5 milliliters) Tabasco sauce, and 1 gallon (3.8 liters) water. Paint this on the tree trunks to prevent munching. This will not harm the trees.
- Set old leather shoes (from a secondhand shop) around the garden to give it that "humans are here" smell.

Anniversary Traditions

Traditionally each anniversary is celebrated with gifts in a specific material. The list below elaborates on this. Flowers in the appropriate color are always appreciated.

1st—Cotton: tablecloths, bed linen, tea towels.

2nd—Paper: coffee table books, personalized stationery, magazine subscription, scented drawer liners.

3rd—Leather: leather-bound picture frame or photograph album, leather desk set.

4th—Fruit and flowers: flower painting, dried flower arrangement, fruit tree or flowering shrub.

5th—Wood: picture frames, salad set, salt and pepper mills, cheese or chopping boards.

6th—Sugar: an iced cake, sugar shaker, icing set, crystallized fruit.

7th—Wool: sheepskin rug, car rug, tapestry kit, or cushions.

8th—Bronze and Pottery: bronze cutlery or ornaments, pottery vase or lamp.

9th—Willow Pattern China: new or antique.

10th—Tin: trays, storage tins, can opener.

11th—Steel: cutlery, stainless steel saucepans, carving dish.

12th—Silk and Fine Linen: silk flowers, cushions, or lampshades, dressing gowns or scarves.

13th—Lace: table linen, lacy bedroom cushions.

14th—Ivory: cream-handled cutlery, ivory-colored linen.

15th—Crystal: cut glass, crystal lights.

20th—China

25th—Silver

30th—Pearl

35th—Coral

40th—Ruby

45th—Sapphire

50th—Gold

55th—Emerald

60th—Diamond

70th—Platinum

Index

casserole dishes, 54, 100–101

cats, 126, 180

cauliflower, 59

celery, 35, 66–67

chamois leather, 139, 144, 155, 157

champagne, 9

cheese, 2–4, 6–8, 41, 46, 54, 59, 61, 71, 79, 113, 198

chicken, 3, 10, 42–43, 51–52, 74, 79, 81

children, 113, 125–126, 151

china, 101, 110, 112, 160, 198

chocolate, 15, 22–23, 28–29, 31, 113, 152

chrome, 153, 156, 176

chutney, 77, 91–92

cigarette, 122, 126

citrus peel, 16

clocks, 160

clothes, 89, 113, 120, 132, 134–141, 168

coal, 125

cockroaches, 113

coffee, 3, 8, 23–24, 28, 30, 33, 38, 99, 102, 106–108, 122, 134, 146–147, 198

collars, 135, 139

compost, 121, 181–182, 184, 187, 191

concrete, 162–163

condensation, 144, 157

cookies, 25–26, 54, 72, 74

cooking oil, 14, 39, 51, 135, 151, 159

copper, 98–99, 153–154, 189

cornflakes, 8, 54

cornstarch, 12, 18, 26, 32, 42, 45, 49, 60, 136

cotton wool, 76

cotton, 120, 198

crayon, 144, 148, 161, 172, 175

cream, 2–7, 23, 29, 31–32, 35, 38, 45, 61, 69, 134, 155, 198

creosote, 188

cucumber, 67, 78, 186

cups, 101

curtains, 115, 141–142

custard, 24, 26–27, 30, 73

cutlery, 35, 110, 198

D

decanter, 159–160

decorating, 165–166, 175, 179, 191

dessert, 4, 29–32

detergent, 112, 115, 131, 146, 163, 168

dishcloths, 110, 138

dishwasher, 96, 104, 107, 109, 138

dogs, 126

door mat, 121

drilling, 175–176

duvets, 125, 143

E

eggs, 6, 10–14, 18–19, 21–23, 26, 32–33, 54–55, 62, 64, 69, 77, 81, 97, 126, 145, 161, 167, 195

electric plug, 123

F

fabric, 116, 118, 121, 130–134, 136, 140, 142, 145, 172